IT'S ALL IN THE MUSIC

Books by Doris G. Monteux

EVERYONE IS SOMEONE

IT'S ALL IN THE MUSIC

Doris G. Monteux

IT'S ALL
IN THE MUSIC

FARRAR, STRAUS AND GIROUX

NEW YORK

To all the aspiring young conductors
who have studied at the Domaine School
with its Master
and who, in time, have become my boys.

I can do almost all that you can do,
But I have what you have not—the Past,
And a sorrow's crown of sorrow is remembering
          happier things,
For what has been has been, and I have had my hours.

—J. R. PLANCHE

CONTENTS

ILLUSTRATIONS

The photographs have been inserted between pages 116 and 117.

I

EARLY YEARS
IN PARIS

Caro:

It seems fitting that I should write my first letter to you from an old castle on this island of antiquity, where so much of western civilization has its roots and where the surrounding sea reminds one that Monteux, though born in the heart of Paris, is meridional in every sense of the word. This classic sea truly affects one; to live near it either fills one with the desire for a life of *dolce far niente* or stimulates in the beholder the ardent intention to create, to do, to be. The very word "Mediterranean" evokes an irresistible longing for fulfillment that may take many forms. Mine shall be this series of biographical-autobiographical letters to you, having to do with Pierre Monteux, conductor of orchestras and teacher of youth; and of myself, his oft-needed excess baggage; and of our very interesting life together. I shall scrutinize the past of the family Monteux in the hope that I may clarify the genealogy of this artist whose character is so profoundly impregnated with the penetrating light of Provence, from which his ancestors hailed.

The Monteuxs were certainly Spanish Jews. A Colonel Monteux from Toulon, a distant cousin of Pierre's with a passion for family history, has traced the arrival in France from Spain of a throng of immigrants around the

[3

year 1155. These people settled in Provence, many in
the archaic city of Carpentras where one may still see the
plans of the Jewish ghetto in the archives of the *Hôtel de
Ville*, revealing a curious form of architecture presaging
the skyscrapers of today—one home built on top of another to make the best use of the small, circumscribed area
alloted them.

The Monteux family name came from the commune
of Monteux. Once on a day when the great mistral swept
down the valley of the Rhone from the far Alps, uproot-
ing trees, swirling great clouds of white dust from the
roads over olive orchards and vineyards, Pierre and I
visited the old town in the department of Vaucluse. We
had come to this land of lavender and thyme, of rosmarin
and yellow genet, of old castles and older vestiges of
Roman civilization, curious to see the commune which
had supplied a name for this roving family from Portugal
or Spain. To our disappointment the only interesting
things to be seen in Monteux were an ancient tower, in
which Pope Clement V was imprisoned centuries ago;
a magnificent fourteenth-century wall built of great
gray stone, covered with a patina of lichen and soft dust
but in excellent condition; and a large, ugly, ill-propor-
tioned factory where fireworks are manufactured. This
latter source of commerce supplied work for men and
women from the town. The streets were narrow and filthy
and the small hotel, typical of hundreds over provincial
France, drab and sadly commercial. We strolled up and
down the various lanes and passages, our backs bent before the ruthless wind and, at last, disgusted by the unin-
viting aspect of the town, hied ourselves to the hotel for a
pernod, our favorite apéritif, and luncheon. We sat at a
round table replete with bottles of the rosé wine of the

region, red wine from Chateauneuf du Pape, cheese made from fresh goats' milk, long bread sticks, and plates of good lamb cooked in thyme and rosmarin. Many workers from the fireworks factory surrounded us.

When Pierre, introducing himself to the assembly, mentioned that his own name was Monteux, a brown, wizened old man opposite asked him if by chance he was related to Gustave Monteux of Entraigues? Pierre said, "I should say so. He was my father!"

From then on, until the last piece of apricot tart was consumed, cordiality reigned and we drank endless glasses to the memory of Caddy Monteux, to their guest, another Monteux from "Panam" (Paris), to the town from which the Monteux name originated, to France, and to all present.

We then listened to a long dissertation on the youth of Gustave Elie Monteux in Entraigues and Monteux. It appeared that grandpère was fascinating to the ladies especially, with his good looks, the poetry he was forever writing, his happy-go-lucky and carefree ways. When he died at the age of ninety, he left sheaves of writings on the love theme, long and ardent verse having to do with rosy breasts and limpid eyes, the charms of the beloved and *la vie voluptueuse!* when I think of grandpère Monteux, it is with a smile of understanding, and I have a keener comprehension of the artist I have married. With such heritage, little wonder Pierre continually dreamed throughout his youth of an intensely romantic life!

Pierre's cousin, the retired French army colonel, told me in Toulon a few years ago that the family through the generations had always been performers in the arts— minstrels, bards, and strolling players of a sort. In Pierre's immediate family his elder brother Paul conducted light music, café concerts, operettas, and at times vaudeville, under the name Monteux-Brisac (the latter being their mother's maiden name).

Henri Monteux, Pierre's most beloved brother, who perished in the gruesome furnaces of Buchenwald, was one of France's greatest actors, star of the Théâtre Sarah Bernhardt, interpreter par excellence of Rostand, and heir of many of the rôles of the famous Benoit Constant Coquelin. At the time of his arrest by the Nazis he was playing the role of the drunken father in Maxim Gorki's *The Mother* with tremendous success.

André Monteux, Pierre's youngest brother, though a bank employee, spent a great part of his time learning hilarious monologues which provided entertainment for our family gatherings in Paris and Brussels throughout the happy years there.

Mme. Clémence Brisac Monteux, Pierre's mother, was born in Marseilles, as were her parents. Her grandparents were Alsatians who migrated to Marseilles in the late eighteenth century, presumably for business reasons. The Brisac family were well-to-do and rather distinguished in their manner of living, their erudition and elegant manners. We always called grandmère the Duchess. Though very small, she was possessed of great dignity which imposed a certain restraint on all who knew her. (I really stood in awe of her, Caro!)

Clémence Brisac was sent by her parents to the Conservatoire de Musique in Marseilles, where she graduated second prize in piano. Soon after, she met the handsome and charming Gustave Elie Monteux of Entraigues and, in spite of the obvious lack of enthusiasm of her parents for this young man and though both were very young, they married in 1860.

From the day of her marriage, Clémence Monteux was the rock upon which the ideals and aims of a family of six children was built. She immediately started giving piano lessons to the young society ladies of the city, and quickly achieved a solid reputation as a teacher.

Caro:

So many questions! I shall take them one by one until all are answered. You know, Caro, that Monteux is not habitually a talker. He is given to interrupting serious conversations with jokes and ancedotes. Delightful and diverting though they are, it is often difficult to return to serious matters, especially as he chuckles on and on, very pleased with the gaiety he managed to create in the listener. However, after a wonderful morning in the sun, a fabulous luncheon and a nap, we discussed your questions and I will answer each to the best of my ability.

In answer to question number one: no, the Monteux family did not follow the Jewish religion. They were prone to intermarry, and in Pierre's immediate family his brother Henri married a Roman Catholic and became devoutly religious later, and so did his children. The Maestro's nephew, Fernand Monteux, son of his brother Emile, married a Catholic also, as did René Bloch, son of Pierre's sister Marguérite. The Maestro's first wife was a Roman Catholic from Bordeaux, his second a Jewess, and I myself, the "Eroica," a Roman Catholic convert, as is the Maestro.

In his youth, as a boy soprano, he sang in the church of St. Eugène in Paris, where he earned two francs every Sunday, and every funeral or marriage merited an extra

two francs. He knows the Mass in Latin, and often cor-
rects our pronunciation as his training at St. Eugène was
excellent. (I'm afraid he, like myself, a Boston contralto
with a so-called "sympathetic" voice, often wished when
funds were low that someone would marry or die! I once
voiced this wish to my grandmother who was shocked
beyond words.)

He told me yesterday that the only times he remem-
bers being in a synagogue was on the occasion of his
father's death, and in later years when he went several
times to listen to Ludwig Altman, the famous and wonderful organist, play Bach on the superb organ in the
beautiful Temple Emmanuel in San Francisco.

I think our mutual love for the good St. Francis and St.
Teresa of Avila has influenced our lives immeasurably,
and we turned to the Church naturally after a visit to the
Santa Maria degli Angeli at Assisi, one of the great sanc-
tuaries of all Europe, which holds beneath its dome the
tiny chapel built by the Saint and his holy friars eight
hundred years ago.

I remember that Spring so well, Caro. It was April,
the Maestro had conducted a series of concerts in Rome
with the Santa Cecilia Orchestra, and we decided to motor
to Assisi. The Roman countryside, bathed in golden sunlight, and the stately cedars, dark and poetic under the
Mediterranean sky, filled us with a sort of ecstasy which
was to have its apotheosis later. As we sped along the
great Roman highway through Spoleto, and the other
old towns of the region, we spied at last Assisi high on the
slope of the Subasio mountain, the towers and campanile
of the great cathedral and other churches caught in the
rose-gold rays of the setting sun. I remember we were

strangely quiet that evening, speaking but little during dinner, obviously in an introspective mood.

We had formed an image in our minds of the Basilica we visited the following morning, an image of a superb church filled with magnificent mosaics and polychromed columns, and we approached it as tourists, anxious to gaze on beauty, albeit a bit weary of great cathedrals and their trappings. Then as we stepped through the wide portals of Saint Mary of the Angels, there at the end, amidst all the splendor created by latter-day architects, we saw a tiny chapel in its entirety. It was so simple. Crude gray stone from the Subasio mountain, a minuscule belfry, a frontal mural, and a narrow door through which one enters its interior, dark and mysterious. I whispered to Pierre, "St. Francis' own chapel, built with his own hands."

Some force I did not recognize seemed to be pushing me toward the holy shrine. We were both filled with timidity and a strange delight, difficult to define. We were alone, except for a monk in the brown robe of the Capuchins who was kneeling in devotion. The little altar was so very simple. There were candles and a crude crucifix, two small vases with white roses. Our hearts were profoundly touched, and we both knelt in unison as if agreeing that we had made the long journey to Assisi to pray together in St. Francis' own chapel at the foot of the Subasio, where the holy man lived and died in "sweet and noble poverty." It is strange how the Lord's will works on one. We were warm with adoration for God our Father, for the Christ on the Cross, and for St. Francis, who had built the adorable chapel ages ago.

Years before we had spent many summers in the south

of France, in another world of dramatic ruins and ageless beauty, for this was Les Baux, in Provence, a medieval city. It was there, in a small thirteenth-century church, that I listened to the voice of the Holy Spirit and felt the light caress of my own particular angel's wing. Our house was situated on the small Place de l'Eglise. The ancient church opposite stood high on the ramparts of the antique city, carved from the great stone side of the mountain, and surrounded by tragic ruins of medieval architecture. The greater part of Les Baux lies dormant, a starkly impressive ghost city, but the little church is intact. At least once a day I ran across the Place to enter its dim, quiet fastness, there to kneel alone before the primitive altar. Sweet serenity and deep contentment pervaded my thought and being, and many times later I longed for such peace. I found it at last in St. Francis' primitive little chapel.

Pierre and I always made two excursions a year to the Chartres and Beauvais cathedrals. These little trips to God, as we called them, filled a need in our lives. To Pierre, Chartres is like a magnificent fugue with its columns and arches reaching upward in graceful, elongated purity of line to the very heavens. We would sit for hours wrapped in deep introspection, trying to comprehend the mysteries evoked by this grandiose and splendid monument. I lingered in the glorious transepts of the vast edifice, an unuttered song of praise in my throat to the glory of the Father who had inspired men of vision, from great architect to humble artisan, in the creation of such beauty.

I hope, Caro, that I have answered your questions and that you see the reason for much that has seemed to puzzle you.

Caro:

I neglected to tell you that we came here to this enchanting place from Rome, where Pierre had two concerts with the Santa Cecilia Orchestra and where, on his eighty-seventh birthday, he was made a member of the Accademia Santa Cecilia. As two weeks before our arrival in Rome he received the same honor from the Royal Academy of Music in London, you can imagine that he feels very "academical" at the moment.

I was delighted to come here where all is peaceful, and where the scent of the orange blossoms and spring lilies in the magnificent old garden beneath our windows has had a tranquillizing effect on our Maestro. For one week he was in an advanced state of exasperation with an orchestra that loathes rehearsing and displays an aggravating desire to show off in concert. "If they would only play that which is in the music before them, not *mezzo fortes*, not *pianissimos*, not *pianos*. After all, they are Italians— *n'est-ce pas?*—and can read!" he complained.

One musician came to him after the concert, thinking the Maestro would be in a receptive mood, considering the ovation he had just received. Grinning happily, he almost shouted, *"Eh bene*, Maestro, we played, you saw how we played, you heard how we played for you!"

"Si," said Maestro, sadly, *"troppo forte."*

Here in Sicily, with the sea and the rocky splendor of the mountains rising from the verdant Conca d'Oro valley to contemplate as one lies in the golden sunlight, life becomes again possible and conversation relaxed. So let me tell you, dear friend, of some of the interesting facts I learned yesterday between plates of luscious black olives and glasses of cold rosé wine, and while we strolled along paths bedecked with graceful statues of Greek maidens and flowering borders leading to a blue sea.

In the year 1864 Gustave Elie Monteux and his wife Clémence Brisac Monteux gathered together their household belongings, and with their two small boys, Paul and Emile, set forth for the promised land. To all French provincials, as you well know, this is Paris. They had been happy in Marseilles; all their relatives lived there, or in the environs, and their hearts and blood were full of the warmth which only *le beau soleil* of Provence gives to its children. Young, gay and romantic, this son and daughter of southern France had decided that the capitol was the place for Clémence's music, and certainly a man who knew as much about shoes as Gustave knew would always find a place for this knowledge in a great city.

The trains were small, hot and dusty, far removed from the Paris-Midi Express of today, and a journey from Marseilles to Paris was no small event in the eighteen sixties. Can't you just imagine them, two young people of that epoch, burdened with two little boys, all their personal belongings in two huge carpet bags made from brightly colored embossed plush? Finally they arrived in the greatest city of Europe, the mecca of all artists, anxious and not a little afraid of the unknown future.

Mme. Clémence Monteux was pleased with the apartment friends had found for them, and even the long climb up five flights of dingy stairs did not diminish her happiness in their new home. From those fifth-storey windows one had a wonderful view over the roofs of the far-reaching city. This apartment was in the rue des Bons Enfants (Street of Good Children) and the charmingly quaint name seemed to augur well for future happiness. Though busy with household cares and the two boys, she never for one moment neglected her music. With her diploma as *une lauréate du Conservatoire de Marseilles* in its ornate frame on the wall of her salon, and recommendations from friends, she soon procured a few pupils. All her life the small sums paid by these successive students of the piano, until the day she died at the age of eighty-four, helped to keep creditors away and pay for the little elegancies of life so dear to the true French gentlewoman.

Gustave, though charming, was definitely not a good business man. All his ventures seemed to fail; shops were started, but alas, according to him, always on the "wrong corner." Due to a complete lack of business acumen, or perhaps his love of life and the gaiety of Paris of that epoch, he could not seem to concentrate on the making of money. During this time he became champion billiard-player of Paris, and kept this title for twenty years. I always laughed when Clémence, congratulated for the distinction of *grandpère's* billiard crown, shrugged her shoulders and retorted with ill-concealed disdain, "This champion crown signifies only that Gustave spent most of his time at the Café de Suede on the Boulevard Montmartre."

They were happy in spite of Gustave's poor luck in business. Paris was Paris, the most fascinating of cities with its tree-lined boulevards. Here they were apt to meet old acquaintances from Provence, or make new Parisian ones. On Sunday afternoons pupils came to the apartment to tea, and a little concert was given to a limited number of guests. Music was all around them—the concerts at the Conservatoire, and the Concerts Pasdeloup at the Cirque d'Hiver, where the glorious music of Beethoven, Mozart and Haydn was played by professional musicians, all graduates of the National Conservatory. The balcony tickets cost little, and music was a necessity.

Two years after their arrival in Paris, Gustave and Clémence presented Paul and Emile with a baby sister. They called her Marguerite. The little apartment in the Street of Good Children now became too small for their needs, and Clémence found another on the fifth floor of No. 16 rue Grange Batelière. To be sure, the stairs were difficult, but it was cheaper than the lower floors, and it received sunlight all day long and the added blessing of a good-sized parlor for Clémence's Sunday afternoons.

A winding street in the center of Paris, rue Grange Batelière, has two distinctions. In past centuries it was a small rivulet flowing gently through the old town to the Seine, an ideal spot for the women of the quarter to wash their clothes. It is difficult for me to think of this street, with its bleak Parisian gray stone apartment houses and its small *boutiques*, as ever having been a charming little stream of old Paris. On this street once a river, at No. 16, was born one of France's great musicians.

I stress the river theme, Caro, because this seems very important to me. A baby born on a river must of necessity be influenced by it, one way or another. It is perhaps pure fantasy on my part, but I like to think that the urge which continually swept him onward to the new in music, and his unfailing readiness to accept the ever-changing scene as it presented itself, must have come from the stoned-up stream. The fifth floor was also important. The view from the fifth floor windows intrigued a small boy told by his mother to look aloft to the sky where all was beautiful.

Here in this quiet street in the center of Paris the Monteuxs lived for some years before Pierre was born.

One day Paul and Emile arrived home from school with the fearful news that classes had been rudely interrupted by cannon practice somewhere near St. Cloud! It was war, and I am sure you can imagine the terrible anxiety of Clémence Monteux, with three small children to feed. And there was indeed little to feed them with as things progressed from bad to worse to the moment of the horrible siege of Paris. Gustave was a member of the Garde Nationale, and as a soldier fought bravely on the ramparts of the city for many weeks. Poor Clémence searched the neighborhood day after day for food. It was dangerous to leave the children for long, as the Garde shut off a different part of the city every day, and one stood a chance of being arrested if one was apprehended too far from one's legal address. She often told us in later years that these were the most heart-breaking months of her life as food got scarcer and scarcer and at last, in desperation, she fed them dog and cat, with a little rat, made into ragoût! (I am told that the restaurant Voisin in New York displays a menu of 1870 listing similar fare at the elegant parent restaurant during this period.) At last General Bazaine surrendered. Napoleon Third was ignobly defeated and France groaned under a staggering war debt made worse by political upheaval.

Gustave Monteux now started a new business with a small amount of money left from the liquidation of his last venture and in the year 1874, to their astonishment, Clémence became pregnant. It had been eight years since the birth of Marguerite, and they were so sure this child would certainly be the last that they decided to stay on in the little apartment. Life was now somewhat easier, and Clémence had a little servant to aid in the care of the apartment. The new baby, called Henri, was not to be the last, and on April 4, 1876, another boy arrived.

They called him Pierre Benjamin. Gustave was very sure this child would have no more brothers or sisters, and thus he was named Benjamin, meaning the youngest, to seal the fact. However, one year later André appeared, to the consternation of everyone, and he was really the last. (When Pierre Benjamin Monteux became a United States citizen he dropped the middle name, as he had always detested it, and felt that it had no *raison d'être*.)

The fifth floor of No. 16 rue Grange Batelière had become much too crowded for a family of eight, and when Pierre was a year old they moved to No. 25 rue Druot, again a fifth floor apartment.

Caro:

In 1880, the year Marguerite was fourteen, a family of cousins moved to Paris from Marseilles, and from that time Cousin Félix Bloch, the violinist, was a frequent and welcome guest at 25 rue Druot. Sonatas were played, violin and piano together nobly replacing the lone piano of former years. The small Pierre was usually to be found near the door where his mother was teaching, or Marguerite practicing, but when Cousin Félix appeared each week with his violin, the child was transported. Here was an instrument whose sounds soared above his head to the sky, an instrument of laughter and sorrow which affected him strangely. He longed to touch it, to take it in his own small hands and make beautiful music also. But Cousin Félix, after playing, would wipe it briskly with a fine silk cloth kept for that purpose alone, look at it lovingly, and lay it ever so gently in its royal blue velvet case. Even the case attracted the child: shiny black wood, bright copper fittings, and a rich blue interior with a pocket at the end for the silk cloth and the little cushion Cousin Félix placed under his left cheek. Never had Pierre seen such splendor! Even Mother's piano, with its shirred yellow silk front and its bronze candelabra on either side of the music rack, suffered by comparison.

The sonatas played by Félix and Marguerite filled him with such joy that he never ceased to beg for a violin, and one day, just before his sixth birthday, Cousin Félix looked up from his polishing with a twinkle in his eye and said, "I wonder how the little one would look with a violin in *his* hands?"

The very next week Félix arrived with a demi-sized instrument which he presented with a great to-do to his small cousin. Pierre took it gently in his little hands and instinctively placed it in the correct position under his chin. Wondrous moment, to cherish forever! Pierre trembled with joy. His serious brown eyes looked over the top of it at his mother and sister. He stretched his left arm as far as possible, holding it in a more professional manner, then Félix passed him the bow, and he timidly laid it on the strings. A peculiar soft wail emerged from its shallow depths. Marguerite laughed, and with a cry of rage the child threw the violin on the sofa, burst into bitter tears, and cried, "I want to play it! I must learn to play it!"

That night a family council was held. Though Gustave insisted that none of the boys were to be musicians, it was thought that no harm could come from Pierre's taking lessons from his cousin. At that time Félix Bloch was second violin in the Pasdeloupe Orchestra. He also taught

that instrument at the Jeanson de Sailly lycée for youth,
and was therefore a recognized authority as far as
Clémence was concerned. Félix said the boy had perfect
pitch, and the playing of the violin would give him great
pleasure in later life.

From the first lesson, the child was enthralled. His dili-
gence and ardent zeal in practicing gave amazing results
in a very short time, and after one year the boy was sent
to Jules Dambé, then conductor of the Opéra Comique,
whose daughter Jeanne was a close friend of Marguerite.
The next year Dambé decided to present him for admittance to the great Nationale Conservatoire de Paris, the
most famous music school of all Europe. Pierre was now
nine.

This idea was immediately objected to by Gustave,
who would have none of this foolish music business, quite
forgetting that music had helped feed the Monteux family for years, and was still paying many of the household
accounts! Then a new champion for the cause of music
and Pierre's education in particular, came nobly to the
rescue. This was twenty-three year old brother Paul, who
told his parents with great vehemence, "I have had
enough of your endless discussions over Pierre's music.
I always yearned to be a musician myself, I listened to
father's arguments against it for years, wasted more
years in other forms of commerce, and only now have I
found an orchestra to conduct at a café-concert on the
Boulevard."

When told the weekly fee paid for *his* talents as a conductor of light music, his parents gasped in astonishment,
and it was decided then and there that Pierre was to follow Jules Dambé's directions in future. (Paul Monteux
Brisac, in later years, became very famous in France as

the finest music hall conductor, and all through his youth
was Pierre's guide and mentor.)

Caro, I am happy that the Maitre seemed in a mood to
talk of his childhood in Paris, and I think you will be
amused, as I was, by these reminiscences of other days.

"I think my mother must have had a difficult time
making ends meet, as I remember her sitting often at her
desk wrapped in a woolen shawl, a bottle of hot water at
her feet, figuring out the family budget. Paul and Emile
were working, but still our meals were frugal, new
clothes rare, and worldly pleasures few. We three
younger children did have a gay time together though,
in spite of the restrictions imposed by our life. One of our
greatest pleasures was the arrival every Sunday morning
of the bath-man. We would hear the clop-clop of his
horse's hooves and the clang of his bell as he approached,
his wagon piled high with small tubs and tanks of steam-
ing water. Up the five flights he came with pail after pail
of hot water. There was always a general scramble to be
first in the tub. One had to hurry, but there was always
time to make a little boat, and sail it three or four times
around the tub before the soap, brushes and towels were
brought. All three boys bathed in the same water, the
elders having their own tub; hygiene bothered folks very
little in the 1870's!

"On Sundays one wore a different suit with a lace
collar, and if we had worked well during the week, we
were escorted by Marguerite and Félix to Prévot's on
the Boulevard Bonne Nouvelle for a delectable frozen
chocolate in a large cup. Sometimes a hot *brioche* was a
delicious part of this feast, especially in winter, when the
chocolate was piping hot. We would watch, wide-eyed, as
the waiter poured the deep reddish brown liquid, smooth

and rich, from the great tin pitchers. The tantalizing odor made our nostrils quiver and our mouths water!

"Then there was the Coco man, his copper vessel surrounded by tiny goblets, strapped to his back. For a few centimes a boy could drink sweet licorice water from those fairy cups. *'Coco, coco, à la fraîche,'* he would call, and we would slide down the bannisters of five flights of stairs to the street, our centimes clutched in hands soon made sticky by the licorice syrup. In winter the hot chestnut man arrived with his little stove with burning coals, and sweet roasted chestnuts fresh from the country, which warmed a boy's hands while eating.

"Christmas was a joyous moment in our young lives. We received one splendid toy which we were to take turns playing with. This will surely seem a poor sort of Christmas to children surfeited with toys, as is the rule today. We were happy and delighted with our shiny iron engine, red and yellow with wheels of black, and I think this one toy shared with my little brothers gave me a sense of values and also a sense of belonging to a family where everything was share and share alike.

"Every fine day, Blanche, our good *bonne*, accompanied us to the Square Montherlant, to play with other children of the neighborhood. Here we learned many things having to do with life in Paris, as we listened to the nurses' chatter while they darned the family hose. Here, I realized, was a world far removed from the fifth floor of the rue Druot; a world of marriage, childbirth, ladies called mistresses, country relations and city flirtations. A world that my mother, in the quiet of her small secluded music salon, never encountered and most certainly would never have let us frequent, if she had known. I think my brother Henri, who was to become a great actor, was undoubtedly influenced in some way by these afternoons in the Square Montherlant. He always absorbed the characteristics of everyone he met, and made them part of his stock in trade later. As for me, my head was too full of music to be influenced by anything other than a violin."

Caro:

I must tell you of our voyage yesterday, before continuing the story of Monteux's childhood in music. As we have no idea of ever seeing Greece in our lifetime, we decided to visit Agrigento, three hours by car from Palermo. We were simply delighted to see the wonderful Concordia and Juno Temples situated a mile or so from the center of this aged city.

The day was brilliant with sunshine, the sky a vibrant blue, the hills a vivid green, fruit trees in blossom and the roadside white and yellow with a small flower reminiscent of our Maine daisies. Flocks of brown sheep and grey goats with queer fluted horns, whole families laboring in the fields, and at one time a mother swathed in a rusty black shawl with three small dark-eyed children on an emaciated mule, two mangy hounds tied by ropes to her queer saddle. There was the sweet softness of Spring in the air, yet we felt a sort of permanent violence surrounding us on every side in this land of contrasts.

We arrived in Agrigento shortly after one o'clock, and went immediately to the Piazza dei Templii. Here we found a nondescript restaurant we all eyed with scepticism but entered nevertheless, as we were famished. We were at last served an excellent risotto, cheese, and fruit, with a vino rosso Siciliano the Maestro found too heavy and sharp, used as he is to the fine wines of France and

California. Caro, if life has taught me one thing, it is that one is much happier sightseeing after the creature needs have been satisfied. So we were very gay as we made our way up the ancient road of the valley of the temples, the two young Americans accompanying us running ahead with their cameras.

Of a sudden we came upon the vestiges of the colossal temple of Hercules, the oldest of the Akragantine monuments in Doric style, dating from the sixth century before Christ, and we were momentarily speechless. We walked in silence, until there before us on a rocky eminence was the sublime Concordia, the most perfect of all Greek architecture in Sicily, practically intact and full of majestic serenity. It has such overwhelming, grandiose simplicity that one feels positively at variance with it, and inharmonious, and the contention within one is extremely poignant. I know Pierre felt this inferiority as well as I, because later he made only one remark all the way back to Palermo:

"To think that serfs, over two thousand years ago, erected a monument of such supreme and noble beauty which stands there today, in utter sublimity, protected from the elements throughout the ages, evidently for some purpose."

I asked him why he thought the Concordia had been spared. He answered, "That man, if it is within his possibility, should see himself in other perspective."

This was the mature Monteux speaking, Caro. Now we will return to the child who became the wise, ageless man gazing at the Concordia with a sort of philosophical resignation, and he will tell us of the first momentous day in his life in music, in his own words:

"The Conservatoire Nationale de Paris has always

been considered one of the finest schools of music and drama in the world. Students come from all over France and its colonies, and two places were kept free in each class for strangers; that is to say, student musicians from other countries. In this category, during my eleven years there, were such violin pupils as Carl Flesch, Fritz Kreisler, Georges Enesco, and Jacques Thibaud. Among the French composers were Maurice Ravel, Florent Schmidt, Claude Debussy, Louis Aubert, and many others of exceptional talent. The director at that time was Ambroise Thomas, composer of the popular operas *Mignon* and *Hamlet.*

"Professor Dambé decided that I should be presented at the famous school when I was nine. If I live to be a hundred, I shall never forget that day in my life in music. My mother had a new bonnet for the occasion, trimmed with velvet pansies, lilac ribbon, and two small ostrich feathers. With the silk ribbons tied in a fetching bow under her chin, I thought her very elegant. I had a new suit made from my sister Marguerite's best dress, red striped stockings and high shoes with pearl buttons. I took my place with two hundred applicants, each with an instrument under a small arm, each a bit nervous and worried, as you can well imagine. Professor Dambé counselled me to be calm, and above all, to have *cour*AGE, accent on the last syllable. This good advice he repeated over and over, adding to my apprehension. At last the fateful moment arrived, and I stepped forth and played the first movement of the seventh concerto of de Beriot. Then came a rigorous session of sight-reading on my violin. It suffices to say that ten applicants were chosen from the two hundred, and I entered the preparatory class of Jules Garcin!"

The famous French teacher of violin, Jules Boucherit, at a banquet of the First Prize Society of the Conservatory a few years ago, gave a vivid description of Pierre that day of the entrance examinations:

All eyes were turned toward a little fellow, accompanied by his mother. He was dressed in a black cloth suit with a wide, starched collar. He looked to be six years old. He had long curls, turning from the blond of babyhood to a future black. His eyes were large and brown, with a soft, dreamy expression, and there were tiny wrinkles at the corners of those lovely eyes, which prompted us to call him *petit vieux*. He wore red striped stockings and high, copper-toed shoes. He seemed very sure of himself, and when his turn came for the examination we all realized that he not only seemed sure, but was. He closed his eyes and played his concerto in a mature manner, then passed the oral tests with aplomb, and was elected third of two hundred applicants.

Here a new life began for Pierre. He was at the Conservatory many hours each day. Three days a week Professor Garcin gave him violin lessons. There were also classes in *solfeggio* every day. At home his good sister Marguerite, who had a *brevet* to teach school, gave him lessons in French grammar, arithmetic, history and geography. She was an excellent teacher, and very severe with her little brother. I have been told by French scholars that it is rare one finds French so beautifully expressed as in Pierre's letters. He is a born scholar and thinks nothing today of studying a score ten or twelve hours at a stretch with a few minutes break for coffee, and a stroll in his "Meditation Walk" at Hancock, Maine.

The year of his twelfth birthday, many events happened which completely changed the family life. Félix and Marguerite insisted on marrying. They were second cousins, and no one in the family approved the marriage.

A few days later Paul announced his intention of marrying his first cousin, Berthe Monteux from Nîmes! The family arguments can well be imagined. The lovers won the day, however, and a double wedding took place at the Temple of the rue de la Victoire, in the Spring of 1887.

A few months after this great event, Emile, who had been travelling in Lorraine, came home with the announcement that he and a young lady of fine family and a large *dot*, from that eastern province of France, named Rosalie Hirsch, would marry that Fall. Thus the three older children married within a few months, and the home seemed depopulated and lonely.

Marguerite and Félix moved to Passy. This was the first *grande tristesse* of Pierre's life. This dearest of sisters had been as a mother to him, thoughtful and tender; her comprehension of this sensitive boy had been of infinite comfort for twelve years. Now she was leaving the home. His heart seemed as if to burst with the pain of jealousy at the idea of his Marguerite belonging to someone else, even Félix. He saved his errand money, and on his first visit to the house in Passy presented her, with great formality, a small bouquet of lilies of the valley which denoted happiness, and a spray of forget-me-nots for sentiment.

From rue Druot the now greatly reduced family moved to the Faubourg Montmartre, then to rue Taitbout, and at last to the Passage Saulnier. Gustave had become a travelling salesman for the Limoges family Monteux, that part of the family whose business was shoes. This work suited his character and he was a success at last! His charming, gay personality, his witty speech with the soft accent of the Midi of France, were of great help in selling shoes to the provincial buyers. There was the charm of staying in a different town every night, and the pleasure of meeting new store keepers every day on whom to practice his wiles.

Clémence found herself alone weeks on end with her three remaining boys. Her integrity, her counsels, and her nobility of character made a profound impression on her children. She was a disciplinarian with a keen comprehension of a boy's bodily and mental needs. I have asked the Maestro to describe his mother for you:

"My mother had a sort of stateliness, though she was a small woman, four feet eleven inches tall. I remember her tiny hands and dainty, slender little feet. Her hair was black and curly and when she died, at the age of eighty-four, it was still black as coal. Her eyes were the arresting part of her visage. They were twinkling, vivacious eyes which could become cold and distant if a boy erred, and she would make me literally shiver in my boots with a look. We all adored her.

"She had many admirers of both sexes though she was not what is considered pretty, but was witty and intelligent. One of her dearest friends was the Abbé Berteuil, who came each week to dinner. A friend once told me he had never heard my mother make a stupid or foolish remark. I must say I never could imagine such a thing, as she was clever and wise. Music, literature, and especially the ever-changing politics of the Third Republic were her chief interests. In spite of our poverty, she was a great lady."

Every year his mother's piano pupils gave a recital in the little Salle Hertz on the rue Cadet. He has often told me of his extreme annoyance bordering on distress at the musical ineptitude of these befrizzled, silk and satin bedecked pupils, with their complete lack of talent, and of becoming absolutely wretched at the sight of his dear mother's vexation over their performance. He vowed, then and there, to be a *real* musician in every sense of the word, to make as perfect music as was within his possibility, and thus repay her in part for these hours of professional anguish.

Cara:

   As we are approaching the momentous drama of Easter, and as our minds are full of these holy hours, I must tell you what happened here yesterday in Palermo, before going on with our Monteux story.

   The day was cool, great gray clouds gathered and dispersed over the Conca d'Oro and the sun played hide and seek, giving our immediate world a magnificent dramatic appearance. We decided to make our usual pilgrimage to Monreale, the most beautiful Norman church in Italy.

   It contains an enormous figure of Christ in the apse, Byzantine in character, made wholly of mosaic (I am told that the face alone is nine feet in height). It dominates the great church, and all who step within its portals. If one turns to the right, His regard is full of tender solicitude for the beholder, and one feels instinctively the urge to kneel and receive His blessing. From the front, He has the forbidding air of a great and noble prophet of early Biblical times. With His uplifted hands, He is the Teacher, majestic in sublime Verity. His strong, compassionate figure seems full of concern for the poor creature small and insignificant, standing with uplifted face there below. We lingered there awhile and then returned to the

Villa Igeia quietly, each occupied with his own grave thoughts.

That evening after dinner, the Maestro was in a retrospective mood, and told me in detail of the first years at the Conservatoire Nationale, over our coffee:

"There were six classes of violin; two preparatory and four superior. I stayed five years in Professor Garcin's class and at the same time was a student of harmony and *solfeggio* in the class of the great Professor Albert Lavignac."

(Yes, Caro, the famous Lavignac of the Dictionnaire de la Musique one finds in every serious music student's library. I have been told Pierre and his friend Louis Aubert, who later became a fine composer, were always the leaders in the Music Dictation classes. While the teacher played the melody, these musical prodigies would fill in the whole accompaniment, to the astonishment of the class, all struggling with the simple air. All music seemed facile and natural to Pierre and the facts of music lay deep in his nature.)

"I was five years under the tutelage of Albert Lavignac, and I assure you both harmony and *solfeggio* were literally plumbed to their depths. It pains me to say there is a serious lack of such training in the United States, and I am shocked by this lacuna in musical training of my pupils. I have had many men with Doctor's and Master's degrees from music colleges as students at the Domaine School of Conductors, yet they could not write a simple melody in the viola clef from dictation or, even worse, follow in dictation a simple line of chant. They do not hear wrong notes in the harmony while conducting, and nothing is corrected. The poor composer and his composition suffer, and the listener is cheated. As they do not realize their weakness, they go on, blandly satisfied with their own ineptitude. This deficiency, I notice, does not appear in my Canadian pupils from the Quebec and Montreal Conservatories of Music.

"I knew I would be a conductor of orchestras at a very early age. I was eleven when I decided this. I loved my violin, but I loved the orchestra still more. In my twelfth year, a great ball was given in Paris for a certain charity, and many composers of the epoch were invited to conduct one of their dance compositions. Among these were the famous Waldteufel, of waltz fame; August Bosc, composer of *Rose Mousse* and other famous dance music, then director of the Bal Tabarin; also my brother, Monteux Brisac. From the age of ten I was continually amusing myself by writing dance music. I later wrote a complete opera and other works which have never been played, alas! For this grand occasion I composed a droll sort of polka on the notes sol-fa-si-la-si-re, which if quickly said becomes '*Sol facile à cirer,*' or in translation, 'Floor easy to polish.' My brother Paul proposed to the committee that I conduct this great composition, to which they readily agreed. You can imagine my excitement."

This was the first time that Pierre ever conducted. I have been told that he and the polka, which he had orchestrated himself for a complete dance orchestra of that period, consisting of fifty or so musicians, had a huge success. I think he must have looked adorable, Caro, in his high buttoned shoes, red striped stockings and blue velvet suit with wide lace collar, bought for the occasion at the Galeries Lafayette. He really was the "*choux-choux des dames*" (little cabbage for the ladies), he says! I must say, I think he still is.

Later while playing second violin at the Folies

Bergères, the assistant conductor of their small orchestra, Monsieur Henri Hambourg, used a stirring *Galop* the young Monteux had written for an exciting act:

STUPENDOUS GIANT HERCULES

IN HIS PRODIGIOUS

TOUR DE FORCE OF WEIGHT-LIFTING

Pierre played second violin at the Folies for two years, from the age of fourteen until the end of his sixteenth year. The orchestra consisted of two first violins, two second violins, one 'cello, one bass, one flute, one oboe, one trumpet, one trombone, and drums. It was considered sufficient, and made an excellent ensemble for light music. His life at that moment consisted of rising very early, practicing his violin for two hours before running off to the Conservatoire, where he spent the day in various classes, racing home to practice two more hours before the family dinner, then dashing over the street to the stage door of the theatre, there to play until midnight, and very often later. I must explain that Pierre's family had moved to the Passage Saulnier, directly opposite the Folies Bergères. Their apartment on the third floor was much larger than the old apartment on the rue Taitbout. As the rent was higher, Pierre felt that he should work and pay his mother board, as did his brother Henri, who was at the Conservatoire also, in the school of drama.

Monsieur Léon Désorme, the first conductor and musical director of the Folies Bergères, not only enjoyed playing quartets on free afternoons, but saw to it that all music chosen for the revues in his theatre was of good light character, and never vulgar. Consequently Pierre never wearied of it. Many years later, in a conversation with the late George Gershwin, who had complimented him on his marvellous rhythmic sense, he remarked with a smile, "*Oui,* my two years at the Folies has a great deal to do with it. There were many dancing and acrobatic acts, in which, as you know, the rhythm is marked and extremely precise. It was excellent training for a young musician."

This experience stood him in good stead later, when as a conductor of the Ballet Russe under Serge Diaghilev, he triumphed in the works of Igor Stravinsky and Maurice Ravel. He often says that he learned many important things at the Folies Bergères, and counsels his pupils to conduct road shows whenever possible. To quote him directly:

"I not only learned how to accompany a danseuse, but I certainly learned much about women from these hard-working, kindly artists of that Parisian revue. I think this work did me no harm, and at least I was helping my mother. I'll have to admit that my innocence was greatly impaired though, and I think with mixed feelings of a certain Georgette with blond hair and blue eyes and a come-hither walk, in whose lovely arms I became a man. Ha, ha!

"I was fifteen years old when I received my first medal for violin. At that time Professor Garcin was promoted professor of a superior class. I competed for a place in this class and though I received the first medal under Garcin's tutelage, I was not taken. I have never known why, but in all probability the good professor did not think too much of my talent, or perhaps [chuckle] he had had enough of me. At any rate, Professor Maurin, one of the finest teachers of the superior class said to him, 'You don't want Monteux? Well, I do, and I'll gladly take him.'

"Professor Maurin lived in a nice apartment at 72 rue Blanche, smelling of garlic and full of cats, which I loved to visit. I often went there for my lessons, and enjoyed myself immensely in the rather lax bohemian atmosphere. I received my *premier accessit* due to the good professor's teaching, and a year after, my second prize, won with a brilliant playing I thought (ha, ha) of one of the last Kreutzer Concerti. I was very fond of Professor Maurin, who hailed from the Midi of France, and the hours spent in the apartment, so full of the pungent odors redolent of the southland are a vivid memory. You can imagine my desolation when he died very suddenly one day.

"His place was filled by Professor Henri Berthelier, *solo violon* of the Paris Opéra, a truly marvellous teacher, who prevailed upon me to work for my first prize, which I won just two years after receiving my second, by playing the twenty-ninth Concerto of Viotti. I was at the Conservatory eleven years in all. I spent three of the last years in arduous study of counterpoint and fugue with Charles Lenepveu.

"As there was no class of viola at the Conservatoire, I decided to study that instrument alone. I wanted more than anything in the world to know the quartet repertoire and to have the joy of playing it in our home. It was really my good luck that very few played this lovely instrument, so I asked to enter the class of ensemble playing directed by Benjamin Godard, the composer of the opera *Jocelyn*, then so popular. Godard was undoubtedly a very great influence in my life. The ensemble classes gave me much joy, due in great measure to his inspiring leadership.

"My idol lived with his mother and sister at No. 10

Boulevard Clichy. These two women cared for him as the apple of their eye. Tall, with long black curly hair, and a dreamy, pensive face, he usually ambled in his walk, and spoke in a soft adagio. His remarks to pianists and other instrumentalists of his classes were both clever and effective, as he was possessed of a profound culture. I loved him with a love I think only possible in adolescence.

"I went to his home to play quartet very often. His sister Madeleine played first violin, Godard played second, I of course played viola, and our 'cellist was a fine musician by the name of Raymond Marthe.

"At that time I was fifteen years old, and you can imagine I was deeply impressed and cognizant of the honor conferred on me by intimacy with a man I so revered. Because of this adulation I tried to imitate him in every way, and to my sister Marguerite's disgust, let my hair grow until it nearly touched my shoulders. I did not cut it, either, until the day of my first prize at the Conservatory. It was a sultry, hot day in July. I passed a line of coachmen as I walked up the rue Richter. One of them simply doubled up with mirth, and bellowed at his comrades, '*Mon Dieu*, regard this one. He doesn't think it's hot enough, *alors*, he's letting his hair grow!'

"This was too much, as there were pretty young ladies behind me, and I rushed to the nearest barber shop, their laughter ringing in my ears, and had the Godardian locks cut. I hardly think I looked like Benjamin Godard though, as he was over six feet tall, and really a magnificent man in every way. I, on the contrary, was but five feet two, a pupil viola player, and anything but a genius, ha-ha! Yet I know that the imprint of Godard's erudition in all things pertaining to music has been of infinite help throughout my life in music."

Caro, to this day, Maestro often goes alone to the music room and plays a work of Benjamin Godard called "*A la Cathédrale*" from the *Symphonie Légendaire* on his beautiful organ which is, as you know, his favorite instrument.

Caro Amico:

I would love to be near when you read this letter. The Maestro was in a wonderful mood, and told me so many interesting things about the start of his professional life in serious music. I have taken down his own words:

"One day my friend Lucian Capet, a marvellous violinist, asked me if I would like to join a regular quartet as violist. The viola was my instrument. I had worked hard to become the first violist of Paris, and later I think I was one of the finest players in Europe. I adored this alto voice. I told Capet, therefore, that I would welcome the chance to play with professionals, and he took me to see Albert Geloso, the first violinist of the Geloso ensemble. I was seventeen and I suppose appeared rather young to Geloso, who nevertheless listened to me play a few of the Beethoven quartets. I passed the severe examination with flying colors; Geloso was very enthusiastic and I was immediately engaged. We rehearsed on Mondays, Wednesdays and Fridays.

"This work and the work at the theatre each night became too arduous, and I left the Folies and Georgette forever. I knew I would never play popular music again, especially that of a Paris music hall. Now I was very proud to make music with these older men, who were all marvellous musicians and fine instrumentalists. Our

cellist was Frederick Schneeklud, a tall Dutchman with a
fine sense of humor. I grew to love him as a friend. His
sense of the comic helped me over many a difficult spot
with my comrades of the quartet in the first days of playing together. I think of him very often in these days of
stress and wish the sense of the ridiculous was possessed
by more people. A good laugh is very important in certain situations.

"We soon became well known and popular. One of our
most interesting and lucrative engagements took place
every fifteen days at the Society called La Trompette.
These concerts were given in the Society's own hall. La
Trompette had an excellent reputation and many composers wrote works which were premiered there. It was
here I met the great Camille Saint-Saëns for the first
time. Our quartet, with the addition of a contrabasse
and piano, played his septet with trumpet, with the composer as pianist. Later I had the fun of playing the
Carnival des Animaux, also written for the Society.

"Saint-Saëns, a marvellous pianist, at that time organist at the church of the Madeleine, was extremely popular.
He played both works with us, and I was very excited by
these two events.

"We very often played in many of the great and
famous houses of France. In the magnificent old draw-
ing-rooms of the France of other days, one had a feeling
of a deep sense of history. To certain houses came men
whose very word affected the destiny of Europe. They
listened to the quartets with a vaguely preoccupied air,
basking in the smiles of lovely, exquisite ladies of the
Faubourg St. Germain, surrounded by Gobelin tapestries
on panelled walls, rose-garlanded Aubusson carpets on
polished parquetry floors, and delicate brocades and

petit point on period furniture. I was deeply impressed by all this elegance and splendor. This was the ideal life, as far as I was concerned. I felt at ease and somehow fulfilled by the beauty of the music I adored, and the harmonious surroundings." (He is still extremely elegant in his tastes, Caro, as you well know.)

"We travelled extensively over France and very often went to Germany, Austria and the Low Countries. Once when I was fifteen I assembled a group of older players into a small chamber orchestra and toured the principal cities of France. Our pianist was Alfred Cortot, who I believe was twelve years old at the time. Although very dignified while conducting the concerts, I'm afraid the great attraction of that voyage was the pretty girls we saw on the station platforms. As the trains rumbled through provincial towns we amused ourselves by throwing kisses to these young females, and shouting unprintable foolishness, ha-ha! Both Cortot and I were noticed, however, by the Paris press, and we felt like great and famous artists, though we were very young.

"It was as a violist (altist) though, and especially violist of the Geloso Quartet that I made an impression on musical Paris. I will tell you of an experience I had with our great composer, Camille Saint-Saëns, a few years later. I was twenty.

"I remember very well this evening in the home of one of the Princesses of the Boulevard St. Germain, where we played. It was the kind of occasion on which the young Marcel Proust might have been present. An orchestra and chorus had been engaged to perform the latest work of Saint-Saëns. There was a beautiful little pipe organ in the large and ornate ballroom, gold and white, with lovely, graceful pipes reaching to the ceiling.

The master had planned to conduct the oratorio, *La Lyre et la Harpe*, and had engaged an organist from one of the Paris churches to play the part for that instrument we were sure he had written for himself. As the rehearsal progressed, the Maître became extremely nervous and irritable, and his sharp, sarcastic remarks to the organist in particular, caused the fellow to make mistake after mistake. Saint-Saëns, at last beside himself with vexation, threw down the baton and cried, 'Is there anyone here able to conduct this work from sight?' The whole orchestra answered with one voice, '*Oui*—Monteux!'

"I had never seen the work before, but as the Maître took his place at the organ, after unceremoniously dismissing his offending predecessor, I decided to dare and do. Before many minutes I was mentally thanking Lavignac and Lenepveu for the months and years of sight-reading I had 'endured' at the Conservatoire. I must say I have had many occasions to thank them during the seasons I played so much avant-garde music. At any rate, the Master was pleased with me, and the concert was a rousing success. The Princess was furious though, as she had engaged the Maître as composer-conductor, not as organist. As for me, alas, I received no added fee, and no congratulations from the lady. *C'est la vie!*

"Saint-Saëns always insisted everyone played everything too fast, but he, who had a technique which knew no difficulties, played faster than anyone. Only once do I remember his playing too slow. This was at Dieppe, a few years later, where I was conductor of the Casino summer concerts. I had a beautiful orchestra there, made up of the finest French musicians, and the concerts were very serious and very famous. For a time Jacques Thibaud was the violon solo. All the great artists of the day played at these concerts. One day I received a letter from Saint-Saëns saying he had a desire to play the Schumann Piano Concerto with me. He knew 'Dieppe had a fine orchestra and a pretty good conductor.' His one stipulation was 'No advertising, as there would be too many people in the hall, and it would be too crowded and hot!' I answered I would indeed be honored to have him play the Schumann Concerto with me, and promised we would not tell a soul who the artist was to be that week. Naturally, as was to be expected, this secret caused more excitement and curiosity than if we had announced the extraordinary event. At the rehearsal people peeked in the windows, hid behind seats and doors, and made themselves obvious in many annoying ways. That evening, the hall was full to overflowing. It was very hot, much too hot!

"The master received a great ovation when he entered, and the Concerto proceeded in its usual form until the last movement. At the rehearsal the master had said, 'You know, Monteux, this finale is, after all, romantic. Indeed, the whole concerto fairly breathes of Spring, love, Goethe. Everyone plays it too fast.'

"I not knowing the tempo he would take, said, '*Mon cher Maître*, I beg of you, play it as you will.'

"He then played it a bit slower than is usual, which did not astonish me too much. But at the concert you can imagine my surprise when, with what I thought a wicked, sardonic smile, he proceeded to play the movement, which is marked *allegro vivace* by Robert Schumann, in an *andante moderato* tempo! We could hardly keep our faces straight and some of the musicians at the back desks laughed behind their music wholeheartedly. However, the player was Saint-Saëns, France's most distinguished composer, and the public gave him the largest acclamation of the season.

"I think it regrettable that many of the truly fine works of the Maître are so seldom played, if at all. The Second Symphony is a little gem, and of course the Third, which is played by certain conductors once in awhile, is grandiose in its conception and in its employment of the organ. There are *Les Airs de Ballet,* the Concertos for piano, violin and 'cello, the *Poèmes Symphoniques, Le Rouet d'Omphale, Phaeton, Danse Macabre,* the *Jeunesse d'Hercule* and the colorful *Suite Algérien.* One might say that Saint-Saëns is the father of the French *poème symphonique.* It is truly frightening the way the symphonic repertoire is truncated year after year of many fine works which in times past were loved and appreciated by generations of concert-goers. Today the conductor of orchestras scans his music library catalogue, and such composers as Liszt, Glazounov, Moussorgsky, Liadov, Scriabine, Borodin, Lalo, Saint-Saëns, Massenet, Grieg, and others are all considered *démodés,* old-fashioned. *C'est bien triste, la mentalité d'aujourdhui,* and I must confess I am as guilty in this as are my colleagues. We are all afraid to be called old style. This state of affairs in the concert halls worries me, as I feel the youth of today have a right to know *all* music. They are cheated of a vast repertoire which, of course, they may not like, but which is a valiant part of music history. My good friend, Arthur Fieldler, has done much to remedy this sad situation and I am very thankful to him."

Caro:

Fortunately, for you, dear friend, the weather has been gray these past few days and we have spent much time on the enclosed terrace, talking. Tonight there was a new moon. My grandfather, Walter Roundy Hodgkins, often remarked when cloudy skies prevailed during the new moon's advent, that this moon is having a difficult birth! I like this pale crescent in the sky above Sicily. It gives me a feeling of renewal, which I hope will have a salutary effect on our correspondence. Now I shall let Monteux tell you of his first years at the Colonne Orchestra in Paris, just as he told it to me :

"The year of my eighteenth birthday, I heard there was to be a *concours* for the place of first viola at the Colonne Orchestra. Everyone seemed to think I would win if I applied for membership in the orchestra, as by that time the viola had truly become my instrument. Though I was very young, I had acquired a serious reputation as a first-rate altist. There were two examinations to pass; the first, before the conductor Edouard Colonne and the orchestra committee, thus ensuring membership in the ensemble. The second, a competition between all the violas in the orchestra, which I passed with flying colors.

"This was a very serious post for a young man of my years and certainly one of the most important posts in the European music world, as Les Concerts Colonne were an orchestra of one hundred and four fine musicians from the conservatories of France, Belgium and Italy, the greater part laureates from our magnificent national school of music. I was, of course, elated, and my family were bursting with pride. I was still a student at the Conservatoire, a student of violin, earning my bread and butter with the viola!

"Edouard Colonne, the conductor of the orchestra he had formed and which bore his name, was a man fifty-five years old at the time of my admittance to the orchestra. With his white hair and white, square-cut beard, he was a striking figure of a conductor. As a person, he was extremely disagreeable. I never once saw him, in the seventeen years I was with the orchestra, make a really kind and affectionate gesture toward anyone. He could be very affable and cordial, if necessary to gain his end (as have been many other men I have met over the years, I am sad to say). He was an excellent musician with fine taste, and I admired this mark of distinction in him, but I could not admire the mechanics of his conducting; his arm was heavy, lacking the natural flexibility of the born conductor to convey every phrase of the music to his ensemble. He had no facility of expression with his arms and hands.

"As a young man, he had been a great admirer of Hector Berlioz. He had known Berlioz, and had seen him conduct his works at the Opéra and at the Conservatoire and was most thoroughly impregnated with the interpretations and wishes of this extraordinary composer. Colonne was therefore famous for his vivid and authentic presentations of Hector Berlioz's works. I feel I gained real insight into Berlioz's music through Colonne's comprehension and passion for this great French Composer's scores.

"I have never forgotten the 'Berlioz way,' though I feel it is music which may be freely interpreted according to the conductor's idea of it. The conductor's temperament of necessity plays a major part in the interpretation. In my case I feel I have been greatly influenced, through Colonne, by Hector Berlioz himself. One might say I received my Berlioz training from the original source.

"I always had the impression Colonne did not like me,

though I knew he appreciated me as his first viola. He knew that my reputation as a musician and instrumentalist was a solid one among musicians. The year I postulated for the place of assistant conductor, which I won, due to the votes of my comrades of the orchestra, he was particularly disagreeable and told me with obvious resentment and asperity that he had not given me his vote! I knew that Mme. Edouard Colonne once made the remark at a meeting of the committee, 'Keep an eye on the little Monteux. He seldom speaks, but he thinks a lot, nonetheless. (*Il ne parle pas beaucoup, mais il ne pense pas moins.*) '

"The truth of the matter is that I was bored to death by the long discussions of the committee on the placement in the programs of advertisements for *Bon-Ton* corsets, a face-powder called *Poudre de Riz,* Pinaud's *Tonique,* and what have you. So I sat and thought of my music, and of the notes I had written in my scores of the various ways Colonne exposed Berlioz's desires, all of which pleased me. I am desolate when I consider the fact that all these scores were stolen from my home in Paris by the Nazis, who came with trucks and drove away with all my precious possessions. Only one has ever been found . . . a work of mine written at the age of seventeen, of no value." (This was found in Vienna, as was a book of Rabindranath Tagore's poems that Pierre had given me in 1919!)

"During the seventeen years I was with the Colonne Orchestra I met many famous composers and conductors. Among these were Charles Gounod and Jules Massenet. A complete book could be written about Massenet. It suffices to say here that he was brilliant, a great and wonderful musician, a true Parisian and a charmer adored by all the ladies. I admired him immensely and loved his music. *Manon* is one of my favorite operas.

"Charles Francois Gounod was a different personality altogether, and I stood in real awe of him. His fame as a great composer profoundly impressed the embryo musician which I most certainly was at that epoch. These men seemed like giants to me.

"Another magnetic man was Arthur Nikisch, the marvellous Hungarian conductor, who came to the Châtelet Theatre as guest conductor every year or so. He was fascinatingly romantic, with burning eyes and exquisitely beautiful hands we were all sure had been whitened, and on which he wore a magnificent ring containing a large black pearl of great value. He was adored by the ladies of Paris, and his conquests of the feminine heart both in Europe and America are well known.

"Nikisch, who was my ideal as a conductor, often played the works of Tschaikowsky, especially the *Pathétique* symphony, which he undoubtedly felt deeply. He was a natural born conductor and held sway over orchestra and public alike, the latter hailing him with great ovations wherever he conducted. Colonne, always a bit jealous of these stars of the baton, remarked ironically, 'Ah oui, I know very well why Tschaikowsky is always played by these visiting conductors. The clashes of cymbals which abound make for a very spectacular gesture. Ah, oui, very, very important for success, very important!' This last said with a snort of contempt. These remarks amused me, but I decided nevertheless that should I become *un chef d'orchestre* as I hoped to be, I would omit disparaging remarks on my colleagues from my conversation."

(Caro, in all our years together, I have never heard

the Maestro make even a slight criticism of another conductor. As for me, I am an escapist; and in all my life in
the world of music I have seen but few conductors in action. These were Toscanini, Mengelberg, Walter, Fürt-
wäengler, Munch, and once at the Metropolitan Opera,
Max Rudolf, conducting *Don Giovanni*, and I remember an unforgettable performance of *Tristan und Isolde*
at the Amsterdam Wagner Society conducted by Richard
Strauss. As I am apt to be outspoken, I feel it is safer this
way. I cannot bear the idea of the "She said——" which
might hurt someone. Then too though my criticism is,
after all, worth absolutely nothing, the listener might
give it a value totally undeserved, because of the name
Monteux.)

"Later in the roster of conductors at the Châtelet appeared the young Willem Mengelberg from Holland. We
were extremely impressed by this youthful Dutchman's
conducting of Bach and Beethoven. Little did I think, at
that time, I would share his orchestral season at the Concertgebouw in Amsterdam for ten memorable years!

"I never failed to record everything in the way of interpretation of these great conductors in my scores. At
home I would sit for hours, smiling over Arthur Nikisch's
interpretations or Felix Weingartner's remarks on the
works of Beethoven." (Felix Weingartner changed many
of the master's orchestrations, adding the sort of instruments unknown in Beethoven's time.) "I did not agree
with Weingartner, and I have never agreed. I have a
horror of meddling with any composer's works. I have
never once, in my seventy years of conducting, presumed
to change one note of a composition entrusted to me without consulting the man or woman who created it. I
would never have the temerity to do such a thing.

"As we were speaking of composers and their works, I must tell you of Debussy and of the time he presented *La Mer* for the first hearing with the Colonne Orchestra, but I'm a bit weary with all these reminiscences, and if you will forgive me, I will tell you of all that happened on that fantastic afternoon so many years ago tomorrow, *chérie.*"

Caro Amico:

This morning the ancient sea was covered with a lovely, misty fog, totally obliterating the far reaches of the sea as seen from our windows. It seemed a perfect setting for a good conversation on Claude Debussy, who so loved the fog-enveloped coast of Normandy that he abandoned sun-drenched Rome and the Villa Medici, finding it almost impossible to work and compose there. We are not in Normandy, however, but in the long hall of the Chatelet Theatre in Paris, in the very early part of the century, a long foyer with two fireplaces at each end, where the Orchestre Colonne rehearsed every day of the week, and where lamb chops and other viands sent forth tantalizing smells as they sizzled away through symphonies of Berlioz and Beethoven, Brahms and Tschaikowsky! I'm afraid the aroma of a small beefsteak, ideal to sandwich between crispy French bread, would evoke thoughts of the inner man having nothing to do with Ludwig von Beethoven and Hector Berlioz. I will let the Maestro explain:

"At that time, you know, there was no musicians' union, and the conductor was really boss! Many times Colonne would keep us until one o'clock, and we would just have time to snatch a bite of bread and race across the street to another rehearsal at the Opéra Comique. It was because of the very full work schedule, our comrades the contrabasses and trombones, whose stands were adjacent to the open fires, profited by the proximity to grill their lunches! I must say these tight rehearsal schedules rather pleased me. I have never complained of arduous work in music; I cannot get enough of my chosen *métier*. It all gives me joy and satisfaction, and I never objected to the long hours imposed on us by various conductors.

"Claude Debussy was considered by all the musicians of the orchestra to be a bit *fou* and ultra-modern in his compositions. Indeed, Edouard Colonne and Camille Chevillard, who presented many of Debussy's works for the first time, very often lost patience with this strange fellow. Nevertheless he knew exactly what he wanted to hear in his compositions. Such phrases as "*Non, non, plus opaque, un peu moquer, gaiment en dehors*, dreamingly slow," exasperated them as much as his relentless insistence that they be followed. I was young, and I found his music subtle and intriguing. I fell in love with all of it and would smile knowingly when Colonne would shout at an unconvinced musician, 'I know it's F sharp and that the G accompanies it! Don't analyse it, just play it, and *pour l'amour de Dieu*, stop arguing!'

"These fascinating sounds, which have now become so easy to hear and understand, pleased me. They certainly presented no difficulties as far as I was concerned. I remember Richard Strauss telling me that at the first rehearsal of *Till Eulenspiegel* the incredulity of the orchestra was so great when the little fugato appeared in the middle of the work that they simply rebelled. Some players even picked up their instruments and left, accusing him of ignorance, and of being a young fool!

"As a conductor born in France, I have been asked to play certain of Debussy's works too many times over these past fifty years, and I am sometimes weary of them. The eternal repetition of measures so prevalent in *Les Nuages* and other works have disturbed me over the years. I am never weary of Beethoven and Brahms, and consequently I have wondered about the future of these compositions of Debussy. *Pelléas et Mélisande*, and of course his great poem, *La Mer*, are definitely the works I prefer. *Pelléas* affects me profoundly; I always feel a keen sense of rapture when conducting this inspired opera. Of course, the mysterious poem of Maeterlinck has also a great deal to do with my love of this work.

"I created the ballet *Jeux* for Sergei Diaghilev, and have a parental affection for it. I never conduct it, or in fact any of the ballets I conducted for the Ballet Russe, without my mind's eye being completely aware of the dancers. Lovely Karsavina, pale, sublime Pavlova, Nijinsky, Adolf Bolm and many others, including the staunch and magnificent Corps de Ballet, are all there before me. It makes me very happy within myself. *La Mer* is quite another thing of course, but still I feel the dance in it, this time another kind of dance, grandiose and full to overflowing with life which has no end.

"I have to laugh when I think of that day at the Chatelet when I first played *La Mer*. We were all irritated by the paroxysm-like sounds we were making, and as is often the case with orchestras, we simply refused to take this work seriously. One jocular fellow at one of the back stands concocted a small boat of music paper. With a slight push of the foot, it sailed on a wooden sea, from basses through the 'celli and violas, the length of the platform. This childish idea met with such success that there was soon a whole fleet of small ships made from all kinds of paper wending their hazardous ways through an ocean of legs, instruments and sound, as Neptune, conceived by Claude Debussy, thundered his way to the end. Needless to say, it was a very hectic rehearsal!''

Many times, Caro, I have heard Maestro say to an orchestra, "There is no use playing jokes on me, *mes enfants*, I made them all myself long before you were thought of. *Alors*, forget it, and let's work!" Only once did the San Francisco Orchestra really play a good joke on him by substituting a Spike Jones record, one of the loudest, in place of the required dulcet nightingale song recording used in the 'Pines of Rome' suite of Respighi. He roared with laughter.

"During those first years at Colonne, there was a very famous Russian soprano living in Paris. Her name was Felia Litvinne. She specialized in the various roles of Richard Wagner at the Paris Opera with tremendous success. I must say that Mme. Litvinne made these heroines of Wagner her own. The lady was simply huge in girth, though at that time the public was not too demanding as to the weight and waistline of a singer. Still it would have been extremely difficult to contemplate this famed soprano as Mimi in *La Boheme* without a smile." (Here he roared.) "One might say she was full of pleats!" (He simply doubled up with laughter.)

"I do not know where she obtained the funds, but the fact remains that she was the instigator of a Wagner season at the Theatre Chateau d'Eau, close to the Place de la Republique, which was completely transformed into the traditional Wagner theatre, with the orchestra covered. The Orchestre Colonne was engaged, as well as two famous German conductors, Hans Richter and Félix

Mottl. Richter conducted *Götterdämmerung,* and Mottl, *Tristan und Isolde.* During this season the great Richter invited me to Bayreuth as first viola, an honor of which I have always been proud. I could not accept because of lack of funds. We had no Maecenas or Foundation in that epoch." (All musicians playing in the Festspielhaus Orchestra *paid* their own expenses. It was considered a great honor to belong to that great ensemble of players.)

"As these chefs conducted three times each, I had a wonderful opportunity to hear Wagner with a complete German cast, and certainly led by the finest Wagnerian conductors of that period. I absorbed this music into my heart and soul, and became in no time a confirmed Wagner addict, listening to all of the conductors' remarks, watching all they did, and subsequently writing it into my scores, which I carried back and forth to the theatre, completely engaged in my work. I was determined that I would some day be a fine conductor of Wagner also, and I have never ceased to study the Master's works; indeed, I know all of them nearly by heart.

"Unhappily, my name is Pierre Monteux, and I was born a Parisian, not Klaus Schmidt born in Köln, and the minds of men are so bound up by the idea of frontier I was delegated most of my life to play the music of Berlioz, César Franck, Claude Debussy, Maurice Ravel, the Russian repertoire, Igor Stravinsky! Not that I do not love the works of these fine composers, but I am sad to have been so restricted in my chosen métier." He sighed deeply.

Happily, time has changed this state of affairs, Caro, and as you well know, he is now considered by the cognoscenti "the great classicist," whatever that means! I am proud to include this interesting article written by

Dr. Paul Cronheim, former secretary-general of the Société Wagner of Holland, in appreciation of Monteux's Wagner:

On the 22nd May, 1813, Richard Wagner was born in Leipzig—150 years ago. This fact has enabled the musical world to proclaim 1963 a Wagner year. It is obvious that the Holland Festival pays attention to one of the most controversial figures in the history of music, an artist reviled or admired, feared or revered, who in spite of two world wars still occupies our minds as a fascinating phenomenon. Is Wagner actually the redoubtable Teuton, the exponent of a mentality that unleashed these wars?

In the Holland Festival, Pierre Monteux is going to conduct a programme devoted entirely to Wagner—a combination which may look peculiar at first sight. However, this affords an opportunity to elaborate this question in a way which differs considerably from the usual commemorative contributions. Wagner himself went to great length to bear out what is generally said and written about him. His work, mainly adopted from German sources, his writings, his autobiography, his epistolary and rhetorical activities, all these factors nourished the Germanic myth that clung to his name.

But we know a different Wagner, an *alter ego*, if we strip this work of its theatrical idiom, in which he was a past master. Then the picture is revealed of an impassioned champion of spiritual freedom, a revolutionary—not only as an opportunist of 1848, but even when advanced in old age. Wagner, forever questing for human values, was filled with a Mediterranean sense of life, aching for the clarity he finds embodied in the French *clarté*. Such a picture, however, did not fit in with the policy of Bayreuth in Wagner's last years of life, nor after his death as stipulated by Cosima, this domineering genius who did not scruple to alter and doctor Wagner's writings and ideas and suppress all that did not serve her ulterior motives. We learned this after World War II, when part of the Bayreuth archives were made accessible and, in 1950, when the Burrell Collection was published. A great number of unknown letters turned up, and other letters were restored to their original form, and we shall learn

more as soon as the extensive study now being prepared is published in Zurich by Franz Beidler, Wagner's grandson, Isolde's
son.

Then it will be made clear why Wagner at crucial moments of
his life sought consolation and deliverance in France and Italy.
Repeatedly he went there—deeply humiliated and in utter misery
as a political refugee, and also when his star was shining brightly
in the musical firmament—and found grace, that is, his inspira-
tion. His dramatic flight from Riga in 1859 ended in Paris; in
1853 he finished *The Flying Dutchman* in Meudon, France; in
1853, again in Paris, he met Liszt and, for the first time, Cosima;
after the *Tristan* scandal he sought refuge, shocked and broken,
in the small, typically French Hotel du Quai Voltaire, shrine of
the initiated, situated in the heart of Paris; and here on the banks
of the Seine, overlooking the Tuileries, Notre Dame and the Cité,
it took him less than four tempestuous weeks—a miracle of
energy and strength—to write the entire libretto of his most
positive creation, the festive comedy of *The Mastersingers*. In
1861 the première of *Tannhäuser* made one of the most important chapters in the history of the Paris Opera. After the financial crash of the first Bayreuth Festspiel in 1876, he went to
Naples and Palermo. In 1880 the dream world of Ravello was
opened to him and there he shaped the work of his old age (the
inscription in the Palazzo Rufolo—*"Klingsor's Zaubergarten ist
gefunden"*—proved that his stay there was not fruitless). When
on February 13 death came, he was surrounded by the glory of
Venice.

It is consequently true that Wagner also stimulated and en-
riched the Latin spirit. In 1860 he was the center of a circle of
French intellectuals who put their stamp on the artistic life in
Paris, among whom were Baudelaire, Catulle Mendés, Théophile
Gautier, Gustave Doré, Berlioz, Gounod and Saint-Saëns. Con-
nections were made which went far beyond casual acquaintance,
culminating in the moving letter of Baudelaire of February 17,
1860, a valuable document which was first published in the
Revue Musicale at the end of 1922.

In this century we can point to Wagner's influence on Debussy, an influence recognized by Debussy in all stages of his

life. The "Chroniques" which he wrote (in 1902 and 1903) for the daily *Gil Blas* in which he spoke of Wagner with respect and admiration were not collected, owing to the war, till after his death. He himself in 1914 altered and revised the book, *Monsieur Croche, Anti-dilettante*, quite a lot; yet unaltered were the passages about Wagner. It is tempting to trace his influence up to the present day, and to follow the development which leads by way of Mallarmé to Pierre Boulez and the serialists.

In the light of history it is perfectly clear that Pierre Monteux, the most French of French musicians, in his youth discovered an affinity that was affirmed when, as a young orchestra member under Hans Richter and Felix Motl, he got acquainted in practice with the Wagner repertory. This experience was codeterminant for his evolution and when he substituted the baton for the bow, he remained faithful to Wagner. Perhaps we have not been sufficiently aware of this kinship. When between 1920 and 1940 Monteux regularly took charge of the French and Italian repertories as conductor for the Wagner Society, he repeatedly expressed the wish to conduct a Wagner performance, preferably in these surroundings. We must admit that at the time we did not see how well founded this wish was, schooled as we were in the traditional concept of Wagner ideology. . . . We are all the more grateful that the Holland Festival offers Monteux an opportunity which was not taken during a previous period. . . . The simplicity, the clarity, the infallible moderation that characterize Monteux are exactly the qualities for an interpreter of Wagner. Above all things Wagner's work, the embodiment of the grandeur of the 19th century, obeys Nietzsche's dictum: "Music must be Mediterraneanized."

I am happy to add, that this Wagner festival program was a triumph for Maestro. This concert was widely acclaimed by the press and the public. I will conclude this letter with Pierre's recollection of first hearing one of Wagner's works:

"I remember the first time I heard the music of *Parsifal*. It was at the Conservatory. My professor of violin, Jules Dambé, at that time conductor of the Conservatory

Orchestra, invited me to attend the rehearsals. I was perhaps fifteen or sixteen years old at the time. My ears had been filled with all sorts of adverse criticism of the German composer; many Parisians called the music of Wagner *les fuits de gaz* (escaping gas), full of dissonance and quite impossible to listen to. At that time, I was an enthusiastic pupil of harmony, and as I listened avidly to *Parsifal*, I found in the music perfect harmonies, perfect resolution, perfect enchantment. To me it was music most wonderful to hear.

"I rushed out of the Salle de Concert, my head bursting with magnificent sound, and walked for hours, thinking of nothing but this glorious music! I ended up in Neuilly, far from my home, and was rudely brought to my senses by the reality that faced me of a long walk home, as I had not one sou for the omnibus. I must say there were many times, later in my life, when at the month's end, if my violin pupils failed to pay me, I was not only devoid of funds but of food also. I vividly remember three very bad days when I did not eat at all."

American Hotel,
Amsterdam, Holland,
May, 1962

Caro:

We arrived here from Sicily the fifth of this month. I am amazed when I consider that we were in the air slightly more than three hours, and yet all is so different. We have always called Holland our *adagio* country. It pleases me to say Nederland, or Pays Bas (Low Country), as it is the lowness of the land below the canals which so intrigues one here.

It is delightful to sit in the keeping-room of a picturesque farm on a polder, and raise one's eyes to the window in astonishment, as a sailboat skims over the dark
canal water above one's head. All is *andante moderato* on
the waterways of Holland, and I assure you, dear friend,
this sense of peace and tranquility is to be cherished. It
is true that the winters are bitterly cold; it is true that the
sun makes rare appearances, and that the damp air from
the canals penetrates to the marrow with cruel intent; but
to one born in the State of Maine, as you know I was,
whose youth had been a continual battle with the icy
winds that sweep ruthlessly down from the Arctic Circle
winter after winter, Holland has always seemed a welcome and rather mild antidote for any *mal de pays* which
I suffered from time to time in past years.

Amsterdam, where we have lived many years of our
lives, is definitely not *adagio* in mobility. Its movement is
allegro vivace, as thousands of bicycles rush by in never-
ending procession. When this form of motivation is
coupled with the automobile, the poor pedestrian literally
takes his life in his hands to cross the street. We are
settled in the same rooms we have always occupied off and
on for forty years. They overlook the Leidschegracht—
a beautiful, tree-lined canal where busy ducks and spor-
tive gulls play all the day long. At present yellow daf-
fodils crowd the banks, and through the brown trunks
of trees we catch a glimpse of bright beds where hundreds
of tulips bloom in frantic profusion on the Leidscheplein.

Close by is the Stadschouburg (Opera and Theatre),
the old Rijks Museum housing Rembrandts, Vermeers,
Hals and other magnificent examples of the Dutch School
of painting and, at the end of the great Museum Square,
lovely and impressive, stands the Concertgebouw (Con-

cert Building) which lodges the magnificent orchestra known throughout the world as the Concertgebouw Orchestra.

Pierre has been engaged to conduct a Beethoven-Brahms Festival this month, and I shall discipline myself and in the weeks here answer the questions in your last letter. Please note, dear friend, the word discipline. The term is exact, because of my "lallygagging" in the quaint streets of this unique city. I succumb each year to the lure of old shops full of ancient, homely copperware and elegant porcelain, blue Delft and beautifully chased silver. I will suppress this desire to meander, and devote a few hours a day to your Monteux story. As we spoke at length in the aeroplane, I will report what the Maestro told me in his own words:

"The year I became twenty-one, in April, 1896 to be exact, I received my first prize in violin at the Conservatoire Nationale. Four of us won the coveted *premier prix* that year. I had worked eleven long years and at last my goal was reached. It was a goal I did not think I would attain, as I had given so much time during the long years to the practice of my viola. However, I passed with all flags flying! I was third, and the great Jacques Thibaud came in fourth. (So much for competition juries, which in nine cases out of ten are usually wrong. Of course it was the last chosen by these supposedly wise men who later became the star. It has always been my belief that the orchestras used in competitions for conductors are the only jury really competent to judge the proficiency of a real *chef d'orchestre*. If the orchestra has respect for the conductor, and his music-making pleases them, the concert will be good.)

"In November of that year, I presented myself to the

Bureau of Registration for Military Service at the Gendarmerie. Laureates from the so-called *grands écoles* (the National Conservatory was one) were happily exempt from the prescribed three years of military service, and were inducted for ten months only. Therefore, on that fateful day, I marched proudly but apprehensively up to the window for registration, and presented my certificate stating that I had obtained a first prize from the Conservatoire Nationale that year. (That great prize, beautifully framed, hung over my mother's piano.) To my consternation and vexation, the hard-boiled gendarme stared at me stonily and growled, 'What proves to me you still have your precious first prize, *hein?*'

"I could hardly believe my ears, and gazed back at him in astonishment and incredulous disgust. Happily, I kept my mouth shut and at last, after a bit of grumbling, he inscribed me: 'Pierre Benjamin Monteux. Born: Paris, 16 rue Grange Bateliere, April 4th, 1875. Male.' This last seemed obvious to me, but I said nothing, grabbed my papers, and ran.

"I was sent almost immediately to Rheims, where I became without a doubt the most pitifully inadequate soldier the 132nd Infantry ever had. I must say I had a few companions who were hardly better. Edmund See, future man of letters; Jacques Fevrier, future composer; Paul Landowski, future sculptor whose works may be seen all over Paris today; Paul Kefer, for many years first 'cellist of the Rochester Symphony Orchestra, and other neophytes of the arts shared my misery.

"I had not been in the regiment very long when our Colonel sent for me and ordered me to give him violin lessons, which you can imagine I did with pleasure. This was one order of the army I approved of, and, as I look back on my years as a soldier, one of the few. Colonel Jeannot insisted on playing everything with vigor, even to the Meditation music in *Thaïs*, which he said should be played with energy! I explained, patiently and politely, that the aim of the violinist is to make the change of bow back and forth without the listener being aware of the movement. He replied that he *wanted* to hear the movement. I continued giving the Colonel lessons, as a welcome respite from routine military life, which I found boring in the extreme.

"My beloved violin served me in many ways throughout my years in the army. I was asked to play at all the officers' parties, and at times we would play very late. Naturally, we received no extra money and to add insult to injury were rudely awakened at the usual time by reveille. I was also asked to play the Mass at Christmas and Easter, and on the whole I think I gave pleasure to many people. At that time, we soldiers received five centimes a day. This munificent sum was paid us every five days. We called it the 'Government Loan.' I usually gave my centimes and also my ration of tobacco to a comrade, who polished my shoes and buttons and made my bed. I was lazy then as now, you see *chérie*, when it comes to manual work. Ha ha!

"Our captain was truly my *bête noir* for ten long months. Nothing could have been more deplorable in the eyes of this army disciplinarian than Monteux at gymnastics; indeed, he spent a great part of his time growling the worst of threats at me as I failed in exercise after exercise. Then too I was usually last to fall in line when the whistle blew for the race to barracks. 'Monteux! Why are you always last?' he roared at me one day when I ambled to my place at the end of the line. 'Someone has to be last,

mon Capitaine,' was my brilliant but meek answer, which
served to lose me two passes.

"One day Colonel Jeannot recognized me while in-
specting gymnastics. We were supposed to chin ourselves
at the bar three times but I chinned once and jumped
down to find the Colonel standing before me, an un-
looked-for twinkle in his eyes. I saluted smartly as he
said. 'I must say, Monsieur Monteux, you play the Meditation from *Thaïs* better than you work at gymnastics.'
The captain hissed in my ear, 'It's lucky for you the
Colonel recognized you or I'd have flung you into prison!'

"I really think I had my share of soldier's life, as I was
called up every three years or so for two periods of four
weeks each, and one of two weeks. When at last I thought
these duty periods finished (I was nearly thirty-nine
years of age), the war of 1914–1918 was declared. I
joined the 35th Regiment of Territorials, that is to say,
of men supposedly too old for the front. However, we did
go to the front lines in the Marne sector, in Soissons, in
Verdun, and in the Argonne.

"My comrade-at-arms was Edmund See, the writer. I
have always been a fatalist and I was sure from the very
moment I joined up that I would come through un-
scathed. I remember especially one day during the siege
of Verdun. See and I were standing in front of what had
been a lovely seventeenth-century church, shells of every
color and size bursting all around us, and I tell you, we
did not feel comfortable. At last See said, 'Let's get the
hell out of here, I don't like it!' After a second of reflec-
tion, during which my eyes had suddenly perceived a
terribly scarred statue of St. Michael through the ruins,
his sword uplifted, in the center of the holocaust (only
a stone figure, it is true, but somehow brave and noble in

its imperturbability) I said without hesitation, 'Why? Where will we go? It is the same everywhere.' Gradually the enemy turned his guns away from that particular spot, and we moved on after I gave my most elegant salute to the good St. Michael. I felt somehow he was protecting us and that nothing would ever happen to him either.

"At one time my good friend See, who was Chevalier of the French Legion of Honor, was called to headquarters and was told by the Colonel that inasmuch as he (See) certainly knew many important people in Paris (because of his coveted decoration), would he please request them to write the Minister and acquaint him with the fact that the 35th Regiment of Territorials were definitely not in their rightful place, and to please have us moved to the back sectors, *pour l'amour de Dieu!* In fact the Colonel was scared, and when told this we all roared with great glee. You see, we did not differ from other soldiers in our disdain of the brass. It was always a company joke when the shells came thick and fast and we knew the Colonel's knees were shaking.

"Oh yes, I had my share of war. I think the thing I hated most was trench and dugout living. The mud, the muck, fleas, and especially the rats which jumped over us in the night. Their incessant chatter and squealing drove us nearly crazy. I have always been rather fastidious, and the fact that I was filthy nearly all of the time made me very unhappy, I assure you. Oh well, all that is past."

As you see, Maître was in a talkative mood (I have noticed most men like to talk of their army and war experiences, and I have always wondered why). In the end, he would say no more and seemed to be lost in thought, so I did not persist.

Caro:

This has been a wonderful day here. I thought of
you and the joy you would have had gliding over the
canals in the Spring sunshine with us. Our small ship is
called the *Marek 3* and our captain, a ruddy-faced old
Dutchman of seventy, has been our able guide to the
waterways surrounding Amsterdam for many years. The
wide Amstel was alive with boats of every description.
The light sculls oared by young students, their bodies
taut with the physical fervor needed to generate the necessary speed to win their school pennant in the June
regatta, rushed by us in bright procession as we cheered
and waved them on to their goal. In the distance the
polders glimmered with the light made famous by Ruys-
dael and other Dutch painters, light composed of a sort
of silvery iridescence most difficult to describe.

The picturesque bridges connecting the banks of the
canals were tended by aged men, old women, or buxom
blonde mothers with fat, happy babies on their hips. As
the customary wooden shoe was lowered for our skipper's
toll money, this transaction was accompanied by loud
whoops from children excited by the sleek white boat
with its gay flags, from Amsterdam.

We ate luncheon composed of sandwiches and chicken,
good Edam cheese and fruit, and Maestro and I talked
of the beginning of the century and of various episodes
having to do with his career at that time. We sailed the
river-canal Vecht and then turned back toward Amsterdam and the wonderful Beethoven-Brahms Festival, in
which he was infusing all the jubilation he always feels
when returning to his old home of music, the Concertgebouw, where there is an ambiance difficult to describe.

It was a day in which we had experienced many joys, refreshing and harmonious, due in part to the lovely Dutch landscape, and the satisfaction of conversing quietly without the incessant interruption of the telephone and other plagues of daily living.

The Maestro talked tranquilly and at great length, instigated I am sure by the quiet, untroubled waters and their *vis medicatrix naturae.*

"As you are a woman, *chérie,* and have never experienced military service, you cannot know the joyous, exhilarating relief of a soldier returning to civilian life. It is indescribable, I assure you. The foyer of the Chatelet Theatre seemed a palace corridor to me, and to sit there three days a week surrounded by my comrades of the Colonne Orchestra, playing the great orchestral works that I loved, was like a step straight into Paradise.

"The Geloso Quartet welcomed me back with open arms, and we gave concert after concert in Paris and other cities of France and Europe. I must digress for an instant and tell you of an amusing experience which happened to me at that time. Paul Viardot, son of the noted singer Pauline Viardot, asked three of us if we would be interested in giving a concert in Orléans in honor of Gabriel Fauré, the great composer, then director of the Conservatoire Nationale, and the most adored musician of all the ladies, as he, like Jules Massenet, was a great charmer.

"We talked it over, and decided with great enthusiasm to do it. Viardot was convinced, with Fauré playing his own compositions, 'It's a sure success.' This declaration he repeated so many times that we were convinced also, and looked forward to the concert with interest, because of the artistic and monetary assurance. A well-known soprano of that epoch was asked to sing some of the composer's beautiful melodies, and of course she accepted as he was to accompany her. We three, violinist, violist and 'cellist, played the two piano quartets with Fauré at the pianoforte.

"As was our custom, we arrived in Orléans early, and proceeded directly to the hall. We arranged our stage for the concert, and played awhile to acquaint ourselves better with the acoustics of the auditorium. Then we retired to the dressing-room for rest, and awaited the public, discoursing the while on the full house we would have, the sure success, and last but not least the box-office receipts. (We were not rich, you know.)

"The concert was scheduled for eight o'clock. At ten minutes before the hour, hearing no sounds in the hall, I was delegated to peek through a hole in the door from which I could see the auditorium. Naturally we hoped the small hall, which had a seating capacity of six or seven hundred people, would be completely sold out. You can imagine my disillusion, *chérie*, when I tell you that my eye perceived about twenty or thirty people seated in various parts of the hall, with long rows of empty seats between them. After a few more straggled in, we played the entire concert to less than fifty people. As we had agreed to share in the receipts, you can imagine our disappointment, not only for ourselves, but for the great Fauré. When at last the sad affair was finished and we had counted our money, we had to laugh, there was so very little. The lady insisted on giving up her part (she was well endowed with this world's goods, I must say, in every way!) So we divided the remainder and received five francs each! As for the master, he laughed and said, 'That is fame, *mes enfants*; Fauré is evidently ignored

hors des faubourgs de Paris.' Just for the record, Orléans
is not one hundred kilometers from Paris, and is supposedly a city of great culture.

"And so I passed those years just after the advent of
the new century, playing my beloved viola, an ancient
French instrument which I bought for the sum of two
hundred and fifty gold francs, and which I still cherish,
as you well know. I played in the orchestra and in our
quartet every week, and at other times conducted various groups of musicians here, there and everywhere.
Then after my election to the post of assistant chef d'orchestre, conducted at the Odeon Theatre such works as
Bizet's *L'Arlésienne,* a play called *Beethoven* with inci-
dental music by René Fauchois, *Ramuntcho* by Gabriel
Pierné, and *La Faute de l'Abbé Mouret* of Alfred Bru-
neau. I also trained the chorus for many works given in the
course of the symphony season by Colonne and visiting
conductors. I remember that Gustave Mahler, though I
had trained a beautiful chorus for his Eighth Symphony,
did nothing but rant and rave and did not see fit to thank
me. He was a fine conductor, but very disagreeable. I
have never cared for his music, as I feel most of it is contrived. I conduct the Second Symphony, the Fourth and
Fifth, but I must confess my heart is not in them; this
attitude is unfortunate.

"During the immense Paris Exposition of 1900, which
saw the erection of Monsieur Eiffel's tower and many
other innovations which changed our lives and brought
us into the new century with élan, I was asked to go to
Dieppe, the large and popular port town and summer re-
sort in Normandy, as second concert master and assistant
conductor of the orchestra at the fabulous Casino there,
one of the most renowned in all Europe. I realize now

that this monstrosity which I thought at the time the acme of elegance, was truly the open sesame to the future I dreamed of continually. I had spent many previous summers at the smaller casino of Etretat, a charming quiet town on the same coast, as violon solo, or concertmaster, as the position is called in Germany and the United States.

"The conductor of the Dieppe Orchestra at the time of my engagement was Maitre Joseph Bordeau. The director of the Casino, the most important man of all, was Monsieur Isadore Bloch. I had been there two summers when Maître Bordeau died, and the Maître Gabriel Marié was nominated program director and principal conductor.

"After two years of playing under the direction of Maître Marié, who obviously detested me (though he certainly appreciated my way of playing the violin) and made my life miserable every time it was my turn to conduct the orchestra, I went to the director and asked him to please accept my resignation, as I felt I could not make music in such an atmosphere of rancor and jealousy. Monsieur Bloch looked at me with a twinkle in his eyes and said, '*Mon cher Monteux*, there's no question of your staying with the orchestra.'

"I stared at him in amazement, as I had been under the impression that he appreciated my playing and also my conducting. Then he continued, 'We are going to have a season of fine opera with a good orchestra and great singers, and you, *mon cher Monteux*, are to be the conductor.' You can imagine my delight and readiness to accept this amazing offer, and incidentally you can imagine Gabriel Marié's disgust when he heard of it.

"During that long engagement I conducted *Faust, Carmen, Manon, Le Jongleur de Notre Dame, Thaïs, La*

Bohème, Tosca, Cavalleria Rusticana, Pagliacci, Aida, Rigoletto, La Traviata, Philemon et Baucis, Galatea, Samson et Dalila, Mireille, and an adorable opera by Saint-Saëns called *Phryne,* hardly known by the music world of today. Of course, there were many ballets also.

"Later Monsieur Bloch, a man of great perspicacity where the public and business were concerned, decided to change from seasons of opera to comedy and drama, and when I bearded him in his den, and asked him, 'What is to become of me?' (I had decided absolutely never to return to the Casino under the baton of Maître Gabriel Marié) to my utter astonishment he answered, 'Gabriel Marié is going. It's been hell with him and his tempers long enough, and you, Monteux, will be the first conductor and musical director of the Grand Casino de Dieppe next season, *voilà!*'

"This conversation took place in the year 1906. I must tell you that Maître Marié made the remark later that he had 'plucked a superb fruit (the Casino) only to find a miserable worm inside,' that worm, in his estimation, being me. Some worm, *hein?*" (Here, caro, he roared.)

"I think those years in the Casino at Dieppe, conducting concert after concert, week after week, advanced my knowledge and skill in my chosen métier more than I realized at the time. After all, a *chef d'orchestre* needs an orchestra, and at Dieppe I had one, composed of some of the finest musicians France had to offer. The public, mostly from Paris and London, was extremely eclectic and demanding. As I look back upon that epoch, I realize those concerts were of a very high caliber, and I have a feeling of pride in this, my first grand orchestra, and the fine music we gave to the public.

"You know I have always felt, and have repeated time

and time again to my pupils, that I am the medium between the composer and the public, and in a way it is a worrisome and most dreadful place in which to find oneself, believe me. I must never let the composer and his music, which is of course the most important factor, down; neither must I let the public, who in most cases pay hard-earned money for tickets, down. I must always give the very best in me to the music and to the auditor. I assure you this is a joyous but difficult project. And so I studied and studied to try to fathom the composer's desires and needs, and I must say I am still studying, and at times I find myself perplexed and irresolute in regard to the interpretation of certain orchestral passages.

"The great orchestra at Dieppe was of infinite help those first years, giving me the confidence and enthusiasm of first-class musicians. I acquired an immense repertoire which has served me all these years, especially with orchestras like the Boston Symphony, the Concertgebouw, and San Francisco, which play long seasons of concerts composed usually of three or four mixed programs a week. These many program changes require an absolute knowledge of the so-called classic and romantic repertoire —Bach, Mozart, Beethoven, Berlioz, Brahms, Schumann, and others. To these works the conductor must add Wagner, Strauss, Franck, Debussy and Ravel; then come the Russians and the rest of the French and Italian schools. Once he truly knows these works of the repertoire, he may follow his fancy by adding modern compositions, thus giving spice to his program, and by doing so advance the cause of the present-day composer, broaden the musical horizon of his public, intensify the virtuosity of his orchestra, and incidentally sharpen his own musical sense.

"Music has been a joy to me and I must say I have

derived great pleasure adventuring through new scores, but as you well know, my dear, I have sometimes found a desert with no oasis, and the voyage pretty rough, with some of the latter-day scores I have studied." He laughed. "I will tell you why, some other time. Thank God, I can always return to that halcyon epoch of the eighteenth and nineteenth centuries and rest my musical mind, and I suppose my musical soul. Now though, I am tired."

This was a long dissertation for the Maestro. He has been rehearsing and giving concerts nearly every day here in Amsterdam these past weeks, and after all, dear friend, he is eighty-seven years old, or should we say young?

II

THE BALLET RUSSE:
DIAGHILEV
AND STRAVINSKY

Domain of the Great Pine,
Hancock, Maine,
July, 1962

Caro Mio:

Home, in Maine. You cannot know, dear friend, what these words mean to wanderers such as us Monteuxs. We wander for a beautiful reason, it is true, but home remains the nicest of all words.

The month of July was truly hectic, as we spent the first week of it with the Concertgebouw Orchestra at the Vienna Festival, where the Maestro had a colossal success with the *Symphonie Fantastique* of Hector Berlioz. I was elated, as he had previously made the recording of this immense work with the Vienna Philharmonic Orchestra, a complete fiasco in every way, inasmuch as this famous orchestra did not have the necessary temperament for this work of intense hallucination and passionate imagery. We have listened but once to this mediocre recording, which we feel inferior to that made by the Orchestre Symphonique de Paris years ago, and especially to the recording of the same work by the San Francisco Symphony Orchestra. (Both alas have been discarded because of the newer methods of printing music on wax.) I felt that evening in the Musikverein Hall a sort of reparation for poor Berlioz, as well as an immense satisfaction for the Maestro, as the magnificent Dutch Orchestra followed him and shared to the nth degree his feeling for this poignantly dolorous and exciting music.

Then we went back to London for recordings. The Maestro played in concert, and then recorded the Ninth Symphony of Beethoven. This was a joy, and he was in a state of beatitude while conducting this magnificently beautiful work, although he did not approve the orchestra "set up" and had many tense conversations about it. After that came *Roméo et Juliette*, the rhapsodic music of romanticism as conceived by Berlioz. This was a colossal undertaking with large orchestra and chorus, augmented by soloists, and an off-stage group of singers and musicians. The music is fragmentary, and the great worry for the conductor is the difficulty of welding the whole drama together into musical coherence. All in all, they were seven days in which Monteux seldom spoke, so intense was his feeling.

This was an arduous month and I assure you, *mon ami*, I am delighted to be here in Hancock amidst my own goods and chattels. (I am, after all, a woman, and months in various hotels, however elegant, becomes wearing to one who loves home.) The first day, the forest, deep and mysterious back of Winterhaven, lured us as always. We walked in "Meditation Walk" through green brackens of lacy fern; the white birches, graceful princesses of the forest, welcomed us with shimmers of delicate leaf, and the lovely cheeping of birds made bewitching music. Through the thicket of young pines, glimpses of the old garden enchanted the eye, the roses and day lilies livening the green with small, vivid splashes of color. Here was peaceful serenity, and I looked forward to long conversations about the utterly fascinating years when the wheel of Maestro's life was to turn on the ideas and doings of a certain Sergei Diaghilev from Russia.

Pierre Monteux in Hancock is a very different man than Pierre Monteux on tour. Here in this country town on a sylvan arm of Hancock County in the State of Maine stretching outward into Frenchman's Bay, he is completely relaxed. Because of the comfortable, lackadaisical way of life here, I knew this summer to be the time and Hancock the place for long conversations having to do with those exciting years from 1910 to 1918. They were years in which the course of music changed and received a prodigious jolt. In the agitation which ensued, a great composer was brought to the attention of the world, and a young unknown conductor of this composer's extraordinary compositions achieved in one unforgettable night world fame. Of course you have guessed that the composer was Igor Stravinsky, and the conductor Pierre Monteux.

Today we sat outdoors under the capacious red and white umbrella on the upper terrace of Winterhaven, and as the Maestro was seated like a pasha of old in his throne-like chair from India, I took the opportunity to ask a few questions, though I hesitated at first to intervene in what was obviously a moment of delightful lethargy. Then I thought, now or never, and asked quietly, "What about Diaghilev, *chéri*, what was he like?" No sooner was the name of the famous innovator voiced than his eyes opened wide, keen interest leaped from their brown depths, the languid mood was over, and the conversational ball started rolling down through those years.

"Sergei Diaghilev first came to Paris in 1909. I read about him in the various Paris journals, and of his marvelous ballet troupe from Russia. The Orchestre Colonne was not engaged to play these first representations. I was busy night and day with our quartet and the concerts Berlioz which I conducted for two years, and also had my duties as assistant conductor of the Colonne Orchestra. Therefore I paid little attention to this advent of a dance ensemble from faraway St. Petersburg. Ballet did not interest me at all, I felt it to be a sophistical form of entertainment calculated to fill in between the acts of opera. It seemed to please a certain public, frivolous and gregarious, who could combine the pleasure of watching and talking at the same time, a welcome diversion from an opera that demanded attention without the benefit or solace, if you will, of social intercourse." (He looked extremely ironic as he said this.)

"In 1910 this company returned to France and Gabriel Pierné, then permanent conductor of the Colonne Orchestra, was asked to conduct *L'Oiseau de Feu*, the composition of a certain young Russian composer, little known at that time in western Europe, by the name of Igor Stravinsky. The remaining ballets were conducted by the regular chef of the company, namely Nicholas Tchérépnine.

"None of this interested me; my tastes were definitely for the classic orchestral repertoire, the great symphonies and operas. Frankly, I looked down my nose at Pierné for accepting to conduct for a dance company. To be a symphony conductor was my ultimate goal, the only one I felt truly worthy of a musician respecting himself and his art. I had listened to many of my friends in the orchestra extolling the merits of the dancers, choreography and décors of this fabulous company; raves of enthusiasm, I must say. I was not impressed by their exciting appraisals of Fokine, Leon Bakst, Anna Pavlova and others: 'Magnificent—divine—virtuosi—great art.' These superlatives I was sure were exaggerated and I went my musical way, content with my own proclivities.

"So it happened that in 1911, during our season with the Concerts Colonne, I was told that the now very famous Diaghilev Company with its conductor Nicholas Tchérépnine was in Madrid, and that a new ballet, called *Petrouchka*, was to be presented that season. I was also told that Gabriel Pierné had been asked to rehearse this new work by the young Russian composer Igor Stravinsky, because of the regular conductor's absence. He had refused (rightly, I think), as there was seemingly no question of his subsequently conducting it in performance. As his refusal was categorical, I, as assistant conductor of the Colonne Orchestra which had been engaged for that second season, was called upon to make these rehearsals.

"At first I wasn't the least bit interested, I must say. However, as the rehearsals proceeded, I felt a certain fascination for the score, which presented great difficulties to the orchestra. I decided to do my best and to see to it that the musicians knew every facet of its complicated harmonies. I think the composer, Igor Stravinsky, interested me as much as his music. He spoke perfect French, which facilitated matters, and knew exactly what he wanted to hear. It was a sort of challenge for me to meet his incessant demands with prompt exactitude. I always gave him, and I must say every composer since, thoughtful consideration and sympathy. I have always respected a man who creates.

"This very slight, dynamic man, twenty-nine years of age, darting like a dragonfly from one end of the foyer to the other, never still, listening, moving to every part of the orchestra, landing at intervals behind my back, and hissing semi-voce instructions in my ears, intrigued me. I should add that he in no way annoyed me, as I was by that time completely subjugated by the music and the composer. You must remember, *chérie*, that up to that moment, I had almost completely ignored music other than Beethoven, Berlioz, Brahms, Wagner, Tschaikowsky, and the works of other composers of the seventeenth, eighteenth and nineteenth centuries. I have to laugh when I think that César Franck and Debussy seemed the ultimate in modern music to me in the year 1911.

"After a few rehearsals of *Petrouchka*, Igor Stravinsky declared to Diaghilev, 'Only Monteux will conduct my work.' I certainly was surprised and did not know what to expect, until one day at rehearsal Sergei Diaghilev asked me to conduct *Schéhérazade* for him. Fokine the great choreographer and dancer, Leon Bakst the marvellous scenic decorator, and Vaslav Nijinsky the dancer were with him. I conducted Rimsky-Korsakov's fascinating music for the tales of *Schéhérazade*, music I have always loved, revelling in its colorful, provocative score, and when I had finished, they began to speak excitedly in Russian, smiling the while at the orchestra and its conductor who understood nothing of their language. Yet he knew he had conducted a very exciting *Schéhérazade*, all the same." (A few years after, when this conductor led a stirring performance of this same work at the Boston Opera House during the American tour of the Ballet, the venerable critic of the Boston Herald, Mr. Philip Hale, wrote: "If you want to hear *Schéhérazade* played to perfection, exactly on time, every nuance calculated, by a magnificent orchestra, then go to Symphony Hall and hear the Boston Symphony Orchestra, conducted by Dr. Karl Muck. On the other hand, if it is your desire to hear the same work fairly breathing in each note played, the gorgeous color and panache of the Orient, excitingly sensuous and exuberant with licentious revelry, then buy a ticket for the Russian Ballet and listen to Pierre Monteux conduct this fantastical score of Rimsky-Korsakov." Dr. Muck had programmed the work the same week!)

"Then Sergei Diaghilev approached and declared emphatically, 'Monteux, will you conduct my first series of ballets, namely this *Schéhérazade*, *Le Spectre de la Rose* (this ballet was danced to the music of Carl Maria von Weber, orchestrated by Hector Berlioz) and the new ballet, *Petrouchka*.'

"You can imagine my surprise! Here was I, Pierre Monteux, serious quartetist, and conductor of Beethoven and Brahms, conducting ballet! I somehow did not feel proud, strange as this may seem.

"Well, this first series was given three times that season in Paris. I have always smiled over the stories of Vaslav Nijinsky's famous elevation, and his leap through the window at the very end of *Le Spectre de la Rose*. The truth is (and this does not detract from the fact that this great dancer was superb in this lovely ballet) he was nobly assisted by Monteux in the pit, who played the chord before the last with a slight *point d'orgue*, thereby creating the illusion of a prolonged elevation of the dancer. When I played the final chord, you may be sure, the spectre was already reclining on the mattress placed there to receive him. Ha, ha!

"As luck would have it, during the summer after my initial season with the Ballet Russe, Sergei Diaghilev found it necessary to dispense with Nicholas Tchérépnine's services as first conductor for various reasons unknown to me at the time. Shortly thereafter, I was asked to make the tour starting in September. I requested a leave of absence from the Colonne Orchestra, which was rather ungraciously granted. We left Paris for London, where we played five weeks at the Covent Garden Opera House. The Beecham Orchestra was employed, and a very good ensemble it was. I have always enjoyed working with British musicians, and fell deeply in love with London, a love which has endured many years, as you well know." (He is, as I write, Principal Conductor of the London Symphony Orchestra.)

"Our itinerary that season excited me no end, as we were to go to Russia, the land of Tolstoy, Pushkin, Chekhov, Glière, Glinka, Moussorgsky, Borodin, Liadov and all the other great names of that fabulous land. I had travelled in western Europe but knew little of countries beyond the Danube, and I felt this journey would be of benefit in my conducting of their music, for which I seemed to have an affinity. I was happy to study it in its habitat. Alas, Diaghilev received word a few weeks before leaving that the theatre in which we were to perform had burned. He immediately improvised a new tour which took us to Vienna, Budapest and Prague.

"While in Berlin, which was our first stop, I had the experience of conducting a request program for Kaiser Wilhelm and his court. I remember the excitement of the whole troupe and Diaghilev's disgust with my own blasé lack of concern over the great event. I arrived at the theatre early, as was usual with me." (Monteux is always at morning rehearsal forty-five minutes ahead of time, and as a result the Concertgebouw players nicknamed him the "Night Watch" after Rembrandt's famous painting.) "I was not the conductor of the first ballet scheduled that evening and therefore was in no hurry. To my amazement I found Sergei Diaghilev in full dress, with white carnation and gloves, pacing back and forth in a state of extreme agitation! As he never arrived early for a performance, I wondered at his excitement. The minute he laid eyes on me he literally roared, 'Oh, there you are! Why are you so late?'

"I stammered, 'But mon Directeur, I do not conduct the first ballet.'

"He snapped, 'Well you do tonight. Kaiser Wilhelm and his whole court are coming!'

"I replied calmly, 'And what is the program? It is rather important I know what I'm to conduct.'

" 'It's a request program starting with *Schéhérazade* and finishing with *Thamar*,' " he answered. As my assistant conducted *Thamar*, I smiled delightedly, '*Eh bien, ça va*. I can go to bed early for once!'

"I suppose my Director felt this to be a *lèse-majesté* attitude, for he stared at me in astonishment and said in evident disgust, 'Is that all it means to you, that the czar of all the Germans and his court have made us the honor to assist at our ballet?' Then he smiled. 'Oh, I forget. You are a republican from *la belle France, n'est-ce pas?*' He could be beautifully sarcastic at times, I assure you.

"I could not help thinking as I looked through a hole in the scenery at the buxom ladies of the Kaiser's court sitting stiffly in the royal loge, how right he had been to choose *Schéhérazade* and *Thamar*, the ballets in which naked bodies of male and female dancers abound. Magnificent spectacles, a bit erotic and sensuous. I'm sure Kaiser Wilhelm and his courtiers had a worthwhile *soirée*, ha ha!

"While we were in Berlin, Gabriel Pierné, who was conducting the Colonne Orchestra in Paris, broke his foot, and I received an urgent telegram from the Orchestra to return at once, as of course it was my duty to do. After all, I was the assistant conductor. My friend, Désiré

Inglebrecht, took over my duties with the Ballet Company
and I left on the first train. The orchestra was glad to see
me, and I went right to work, rehearsing a brilliant program for the following Sunday. It consisted of the Roman
Carnival overture of Berlioz, the Piano Concerto of Robert Schumann, played by Emil Sauer, and the Third
Symphony of Beethoven, the 'Eroica.' The orchestra gave
me of their best and I received an ovation from the public. This was the first, and only, time I was ever asked to
conduct a concert with the Colonne Orchestra during my
long tenure as assistant conductor with that organization
—seventeen years! Yet those learned gentlemen the
critics wrote that any member of the orchestra could have
conducted the concert by heart, as I had (no one directed
an orchestra without score, in those days) and they hoped
Gabriel Pierné would return posthaste. *Pour ces messieurs*
I had become a Ballet Conductor indeed. *C'est la vie,
hein?*

"I was really depressed by this contretemps in Paris,
and was more than delighted when within a month I received a telegram from Sergei Diaghilev, at that time in
Vienna with the Ballet, 'TAKE FIRST TRAIN, NEED YOU,
urgence!' So I packed my bags and returned happily to
the Ballet.

"It was in Vienna that I had one of the few unpleasant
experiences I have ever had with an orchestra. It was because of *Petrouchka* and Stravinsky. I have always felt
this work of Stravinsky's to be my own, and I have had
a sort of jealousy, if you will, when others have conducted
it. I still conduct it in its original form, and I must say I
was chagrined and furious when Stravinsky rearranged
it a few years ago for smaller orchestra. I have never conducted this version of *Petrouchka*, and needless to say, I

never will. It seems anemic to me, in comparison with
my *Petrouchka*.

"Diaghilev had engaged the Vienna Opera House, and
I was proud and elated to conduct an ensemble of world-
wide fame there. I was well aware of their historical
place in music, their respect for tradition, and their rather
provincial and insular limitations as far as the world of
modern music was concerned. I have known people to
whom the word *Wien* tends to cause a sort of mesmeric
trauma, but I have never been so mesmerized. The new in
music has always intrigued me, and I feel fine music can
be made anywhere, given the right components.

"Igor Stravinsky insisted on the complete Philharmonic Orchestra for *Petrouchka*. This demand aroused
endless discussions with the management, both sides air-
ing their views in an atmosphere of disdain and acrid
verbiage. The whole orchestra rebelled at playing such
'dirty music.' Then, to cap the climax, the string section
struck! Yes, *chérie*, struck, but in a peculiar way, as you
will see. At the first performance, violins, violas, 'celli
and basses played so pianissimo I could hardly hear them,
and to add to the confusion, the brass and woodwinds
played fortissimo. You can imagine how *any* music would
sound when played like this, but with *Petrouchka* it was a
cacophony the like of which you cannot possibly imagine.
I was so angry I made the strings a sign that they were
still too loud, a gesture that disconcerted them no end.
Then I urged the trombones and trumpets, already purple in the face from their exertions, to play still louder!

"I literally wept for my poor *Petrouchka* in the face of
this terrible disequilibrium of sound. The next day, an
august committee from the orchestra waited upon me and
insisted that their action was not to be interpreted as

against *me*. I answered scornfully, 'Very well, but I assure you that in my country if part strike, all strike!' The result of this meeting? At rehearsal the following day *everyone* played pianissimo, and again I made frantic signs that it was much too loud, to their consternation. Sergei de Diaghilef, who happened to be in the theatre at the time, yelled at me from the rear of the stalls, '*Monteux, ce n'est pas Petrouchka là, c'est une marche funèbre!* It's not *Petrouchka*, its a funeral march!' Well! When the orchestra heard this, they all jumped to their feet, shaking violins, oboes, flutes and trumpets at him in a menacing way and shouting for an apology, immediately! Knowing very well their inability to understand fluent French spoken quickly, he strode forward to the balustrade which separated the pit from the stall and really proceeded to insult them in an extraordinary mixture of French and Russian, calling them loggerheads, narrow-minded nincompoops, and other most uncomplimentary and even obscene names. They obviously did not comprehend, but as he was a good actor and covered his fury and anger with restrained gestures and facial expressions, they accepted this droll apology and I went on with rehearsal. The results were dull uninspired performances because, *chérie*, the great Vienna Philharmonic simply could not play *Petrouchka*." (Monteux conducted *Petrouchka* four years ago in Vienna with this same orchestra, a concert performance, and I must say the spirit of the work was still lacking. Though all the notes were there, it was too carefully played. Even the great Berlin Philharmonic a few years ago found the playing of this gay work difficult. In the second tableau the first trumpet of that famous orchestra had such difficulty with the solo that the management sent to the Radio Orchestra for a substitute.)

"We gave our full quota of ballets in spite of all these vexations, and then left for Budapest. You cannot imagine the joy I experienced as the train rolled on toward Hungary. I could not leave the train window and stood most of the way, so curious was I to see the country of Liszt and Nikisch, of wild players and intoxicating gypsy music. Budapest was a joy for me, but not for Igor Stravinsky, because of the fact that no third harp could be found in the whole city to play the *Firebird* music! An extremely heated argument ensued between Stravinsky and Diaghilev, and I heard the composer of this beautiful ballet say over and over, 'It is not my music. It is nothing but gaveneau, GAVENEAU!' Every time this word made its appearance in the verbal battle, it was louder and louder. When the fireworks had subsided, I told Sergei Diaghilev that I knew that word was *merde* in French. He glared at me and said, 'You do, do you? Then we can speak freely in Russian henceforth, *tant mieux*.' I must say that word had paramount place in many a discussion!

"I was delighted to learn that we would next go to the Côte d'Azur. I had never seen the Mediterranean, though I had always felt its pull, due I suppose to my heritage from the Monteuxs of Provence. The great sea did not disappoint me and I was fascinated by the superficiality of Monte Carlo and its too obvious elegance, an unhappy contrast to the vast blue sea, so noble and grand. I remember my disgust, leaving the theatre long after midnight, to see the flowers I had thought a natural growth in the garden of the Casino removed from the ground in brown earthenware pots by a gardener and transferred to a waiting cart, while others, fresh and in bud, in the same kind of pot, replaced them in the hole in the earth. This incident was symbolic to me of the substance of life in this place of spurious luxury.

"Our performance took place in the Grande Salle (really a small theatre) of the Monte Carlo Opera which was part of the Casino. The Director of the Casino at that time was Monsieur Raoul Ginsbourg, a great friend of Diaghilev. There were very strict rules regarding the employees of the Casino. No singer, musician or dancer, or for that matter any other employee was permitted entrance to the gambling parlors. This rule certainly caused me no loss of sleep, but many members of the orchestra rebelled at what they considered an unjust law. I think this a wise rule."

(It is strange, Caro, that most orchestra musicians have real faith in wheels of fortune, and games of chance. Backstage in all orchestra rooms musicians play continually—poker, bridge, rummy, chess, checkers. I know one very famous concertmaster, an habitual gambler, who has accumulated a small fortune by exercising his card sense during many years of backstage games. I have rarely seen musicians reading a book in the intervals between numbers, although I have known a few to have fine libraries and a profound love of literature. These past years, as you know, I have stayed in the wings during all of Maestro's concerts, and it has been an interesting experience, I assure you.)

"Our first performance of Petrouchka in the Théâtre de Monte Carlo was a very great success, with the elite gathered to see and hear the new ballet. To my astonishment, the French orchestra, like the Vienna Philharmonic, rebelled at the few dissonances and I well remember the first oboe's disgust, and the grimace he made, as he played a certain musical phrase in the colorful score of Igor Stravinsky. I stopped the rehearsal and called his attention to the fact that *Petrouchka*, during the same interval in the music which caused him such displeasure, makes a sort of kick, magnificently at one with the music. I said, 'You see how well it is made. One does not sneer at such marks of genius!' It seemed I was always in some sort of verbal combat for this Russian composer, whose music I had strangely made my own.

"I finished the season at Monte Carlo and returned to my orchestra in Dieppe, thus transferring from one casino to another, each with its own style—Monte Carlo fashionable and glittering, Dieppe an incredible pseudo-oriental structure of awesome bad taste. But I enjoyed returning to a great symphony orchestra and the programs I had prepared for the summer's concerts. What a joy it was to return to Beethoven and Brahms, year after year. Excursions in the world of modern music are immensely stimulating, and I have never lost interest in the modern composer. My musical horizon has always been there in the far distance, and I hope never to attain it, as the journey is infinitely engrossing.

"I was very happy that summer in Dieppe. My musical image had grown, I felt very sure of myself as an interpretive artist, due I think to my travels, work with other orchestras, and in new music. In August I received a letter from Diaghilev announcing his fall season, and urgently requesting my presence for the first rehearsal. I returned to Paris and asked a second leave from the Colonne Orchestra. The Committee met and in a heated session, in which Gabriel Pierné proved inflexible, I was refused.

"As I had made up my mind to go with Diaghilev at any price, I then asked for my demission papers. I was told bluntly by the Committee, 'You can't get a demission in September. June is the month for demissions, as you very well know, Monteux.' I insisted, and was told in no uncertain terms, 'If you persist, we must confiscate all the money you have in the *caisse de secours* (pension fund) .' This rather large sum consisted of savings from my earnings with the Colonne Orchestra for seventeen years! Well, I didn't hesitate one minute, *chérie*. I received my demission and left enthusiastically for the winter tour with Diaghilev and the Ballet Russe, which by this time had achieved great fame in Europe. We made our usual tour and had immense success in every city where we appeared.

"During the London season I was called back to Paris, due to an important event in our family. In my absence, Thomas Beecham, whose orchestra we were using, conducted *Petrouchka* and *Le Spectre de la Rose* with absolutely no rehearsals, thus proving by splendid performances his immense and clever gifts as a musician and conductor. Reynaldo Hahn conducted his own ballet, *Le Dieu bleu*, in the same program.

"I know you are dying to hear the story of *Le Sacre du Printemps*, but I think we should leave that for another day as it is an episode in itself."

Winterhaven,
Hancock, Maine,
July, 1962

Caro:

It has rained for three days, a chilly north-easter. Here at Winterhaven, living becomes more intense, pots on the cook stove simmer and boil, the old house is full of delectable odors, and the Maestro has decided to reread Proust. Late yesterday afternoon the pelting torrent sud-

denly stopped as if an invisible hand had pushed a lever.
After two days of creaking doors, complaining shutters,
crackling branches, incessant tattoo on window panes, the
sudden silence almost bewildered us. I know you will
understand, Caro, when I tell you that this extravagance
of the elements seemed in my estimation a marvelous
mise en scène for a good conversation with the Maestro
regarding the first performance of *Le Sacre du Printemps.* After a delicious dinner of French onion soup,
sliced hot Virginia ham, green salad and fruit tart, I
placed a good-sized log of hard birch wood on the fire
and boldly broached the subject. At first the conversation
lagged, due no doubt to the comfort of a full stomach, the
warmth of the fire and the coziness of our keeping-room.
Then I ventured:

"Pierre, why did you weep as you did when the telegram came announcing Diaghilev's death?" (We were
living in Belgium that summer of 1929 at the villa La
Pastorale at La Hulpe, not far from Brussels. When the
pull-bell at the gate proclaimed a visitor, we both had
troubled premonitions. Guillaume, our man-servant,
came up the path waving the yellow envelope containing
the sad message. Without a word, Pierre put the telegram
in his pocket and strode off quickly through the woods
surrounding our home. After what seemed to me an interminable time, he returned. I did not speak, and he was
silent but I saw that he had wept.) He now said:

"I wept for many reasons. Sergei Diaghilev was in-
dubitably one of the first truly great personalities I had
ever met. He was more to me than my Director. I respected his culture, his impeccable taste in all things, his
continual awareness of talent in others and the fact that he
dared! So few people DARE. Then too, he was kind to

me and most thoughtful. He gave me my great chance and saw that it was not missed by lack of rehearsals. I owed him loyalty then, and still do. I loved him.

"I remember him once calling out to me, in a rehearsal in London in which I had little time, as it was for repeat performance, 'Monteux, that second trumpet is playing a C natural and it's B flat!' Needless to say, I was aware of the fact and intended to correct it at the end of the rehearsal, but I was tickled to see that my Director knew the score also. Throughout our association I was made cognizant of this knowledge of the music and of his meticulous concern for it. He often came to the Majestic Hotel in Paris where I lived in later years and we spent many happy moments discussing our triumphs in other years.

"In the summer of 1912 Diaghilev came to me one day, as I was working in the theatre, and in a rather secretive manner whispered, 'Stravinsky has written an extraordinary new work that I want you to hear with me this afternoon.'

"I was elated all through luncheon thinking, Stravinsky no doubt has reverted to the lovely melodies of *L'Oiseau de Feu* or perhaps even farther. Of course this 'reverting' did not come until years later, in the *Pulcinella Suite*, *Apollon Musagète* and other lovely works. So you see, *chérie*, I was little prepared for the music I was to hear that afternoon.

"The room was small and the music was large, the sound of it completely dwarfing the poor piano on which the composer was pounding, completely dwarfing Diaghilev and his poor conductor listening in utter amazement, completely dwarfing Monte Carlo, I might say.

The old upright piano quivered and shook as Stravinsky tried to give us an idea of his new work for ballet.

"I remember vividly his dynamism and his sort of ruthless impetuosity as he attacked the score. By the time he had reached the second tableau, his face was so completely covered with sweat that I thought, 'He will surely burst, or have a syncope.' My own head ached badly, and I decided then and there that the symphonies of Beethoven and Brahms were the only music for me, not the music of this crazy Russian! I must admit I did not understand one note of *Le Sacre du Printemps*. My one desire was to flee that room and find a quiet corner in which to rest my aching head. Then my Director turned to me and with a smile said, 'This is a masterpiece, Monteux, which will completely revolutionize music and make you famous, because you are going to conduct it.' And of course, I did.

"Day after day I studied the score with Stravinsky at the piano. I studied it all that winter. In the spring we brought it to the orchestra engaged for the Paris season. We rehearsed the strings first, then woodwinds and brass, each section of the orchestra alone, except for the percussion instruments which were there all the time. The musicians thought it absolutely crazy, but as they were well paid, their discipline was not too bad! When at last I put the whole thing together, it seemed chaotic but Stravinsky was behind me pointing out the little phrases he wished heard. We rehearsed over and over the small difficult parts, and at last were ready for the ballet. We had in all, seventeen rehearsals." (Stravinsky has written, in his fine autobiography, "Monteux knew his job thoroughly. He knew how to get on with his musicians

. . . thus he was able to achieve a very clean and finished rendition of my score.")

"You may think this strange, *chérie*, but I have never seen the ballet. The night of the première, I kept my eyes on the score, playing the exact tempo Igor had given me and which, I must say, I have never forgotten. As you know, the public reacted in a scandalous manner. They filled the new Champs Elysées Theatre to overflowing, manifested their disapprobation of the ballet in a most violent manner. The elegant Parisians in the stalls and boxes shouted outrageous insults to the enthusiastic crowd in the balconies. They in turn responded by screaming imprecations both salty and provocative, due to their infinitely richer vocabulary. '*A bas des grues du 16ème!*' (the 16th was the chic quarter of Paris) and similar insults were hooted in unison over and over, causing many a Countess to gnash her teeth over these intolerable affronts. One of my bass players who from his stand at the end of the pit had a partial view of the stalls, told me that many a gentleman's shiny top hat or soft fedora was ignominiously pulled by an opponent down over his eyes and ears, and canes were brandished like menacing implements of combat all over the theatre.

"The gendarmes arrived at last. Well, on hearing this near riot behind me I decided to keep the orchestra together at any cost, in case of a lull in the hubbub. I did, and we played it to the end absolutely as we had rehearsed it in the peace of an empty theatre. After that performance, we played it five times, and five times the public reacted in the same way. This reaction amazed me, as the Parisian usually considers himself a real connoisseur of the arts, adoring everything a bit avant-garde, at times carrying his credulous snobbism almost to the point of sophism.

"We played *Le Sacre* a few times in London to very polite audiences, obviously bent on showing greater sophistication in regard to music and ballet than Paris. Then, as the saying goes, the work was 'shelved.'

"It was a year later, during the season of the Concerts Monteux (a series I gave at the Casino de Paris) I suggested to Stravinsky that I program *Le Sacre* just as I had *Petrouchka* the year before. I felt sure the great work would have a colossal success if heard alone in concert. I had not seen the ballet, but friends had described it to me and I was convinced half the manifestations were rebellion at a new form of choreographic art. Stravinsky agreed and, before a theatre completely sold out, with everyone who was anyone in Paris musical circles in attendance, the work was performed. My mother had a loge and Camille Saint-Saëns sat with her. She told me afterward that the great French composer did nothing but repeat over and over, '*Mais il est fou, il est fou!* He is crazy, he is crazy!' As the work progressed, Saint-Saëns became very angry, as much with me I believe as with Stravinsky, and left in high dudgeon. The reaction of those musicians who had played the première of the work was very different; many said to me, 'That music has already aged.' Ha, ha! It's now fifty years old and I do not think it has aged at all. I had pleasure in conducting the fiftieth anniversary of *Le Sacre* this spring (on May 29th, 1963) with my London Symphony Orchestra, as you well know." (Albert Hall's six thousand places were completely sold out for the orchestra fund. People sensed a great musical event and their response, Caro, was simply terrific.)

"I returned to Dieppe and my beautiful orchestra. *Le Sacre* had made me famous, and the Casino was crowded for all my concerts. I was elated and was making plans for the future.

"There was a dark cloud on the horizon, just the same. In June the Archduke Francis Ferdinand, heir to the Austrian throne, and his wife had been ruthlessly assassinated in Sarajevo. A great to-do was made of this in the papers, but we in Dieppe were occupied with music, dancing, and general summer gaiety. If we thought about it at all, it was certainly with the feeling, 'What has this to do with me?'

"Austria declared war on Serbia on July 28th, Germany declared war against Russia August 1st, and two days later against France, Russia's good ally. By the end of that fateful month all of Europe and a part of Asia Minor were at war. In the Far East, Japan declared war on Germany on August 23rd and Austria declared war on Japan August 25th. These events followed one on the other like thunder-bolts, and within a few days the Casino and the villas were closed, and the summer holiday-makers returned to their homes in Paris and elsewhere. As for me, I was immediately notified to join my regiment the Territorials, then in bivouac at Melun. There I was again, *poilu* second class—only at war this time!

"Naturally, I was disgusted, as were all my comrades. I would sit for hours after drill, thinking of my music and reliving the past three years with the Ballet Russe. I wondered about many things which troubled me during those fruitful years. For instance, Ravel's *Daphnis and Chloë* which I gave in first performance in 1912. At first Diaghilev had been very enthusiastic with Ravel's magnificent score, but for some reason, which I have always thought was due to the weakness of the choreography, his fervor for Ravel and his music diminished to such a low pitch it became most difficult to work as we should have done. All the musicians in the orchestra, and I might say in Paris, knew this was Maurice Ravel's greatest work, and we could not understand this lack of interest on the part of our Director. I knew there was a so-called movement to be rid of Fokine and to replace him by Nijinsky, but this seemed too far-fetched to me at the time to take seriously.

"The season before *Daphnis*, a ballet called *Narcisse* was given by the company and the décors Leon Bakst had made for this ballet were used for *Daphnis*, since it was in the same style. He later created new décors for Ravel's work, but many of the old costumes of *Narcisse* were used for this new ballet. Once Fokine started rehearsals for *Daphnis*, we were all made desolate by the obvious lack of interest shown by Diaghilev. I managed to have the needed rehearsals for the first and second tableaux, but did not have the music for the third and last tableaux as long as I would have wished, considering Ravel added voices to the score at a later date.

"Nijinsky was dancing Debussy's *Afternoon of a Faun* at the same time, and our Director gave his whole interest to this creation of his favorite. That the *Faun* should have precedence over *Daphnis* saddened me. Nijinsky was a great dancer, *chérie*, but a poor choreographer. I always felt his intelligence was mainly to be found in his feet, legs and arms. This was a very unhappy time for the company.

"Later Nijinsky created Debussy's *Jeux* and it was simply asinine as choreography! Much has been written of these momentous days in music and of the ballet itself. I have never been a ballet enthusiast, because it was always the music which interested me.

"I had immense respect for Fokine. I considered him a supreme master of his art. He was easy to work with, very considerate and, above all, exact. Of course, I was aware of the relations between Diaghilev and Nijinsky, and aware also of the cabal against Fokine, who had in a rage accused Diaghilev of this relationship. As I see it, this tirade was the beginning of the end of the great epoch of the Ballet Russe.

"As I have told you, we Territorials were sent to Soissons, then Verdun, and at last to the front-line trenches in the Argonne. Filth and boredom were our lot for months.

"To relieve this state of affairs, I was asked by our Colonel to form a small band with any musicians to be found in the company. We sent to Paris and to Dieppe for old instruments and music, and a curious lot of battered trombones, clarinets and drums arrived in due time. I started rehearsing daily my aggregation of farmers, blacksmiths, barbers and other brave amateurs of all walks of life. As therapy, this was an excellent idea. As music, it was simply awful noise! However, it was greatly appreciated by the peasants in the villages and by the players themselves, who literally blew their heads off in their enthusiasm.

"The Colonel asked me if I would not like to be nominated sous-chef de musique. He did not have the right to nominate an officer, but thought it would be fine for me to eat in the mess of the petty-officers. I answered I was very flattered by his offer, but that I preferred to be a simple soldier. I thought to myself, 'If I am nominated sous-chef, I will be sous-chef; but as a simple soldier, I will be the chef de musique.' The Colonel had never thought of this.

"A very amusing thing happened at this time. One morning our sentinel came to me and said, 'I had a long conversation with the German sentinel last night.' They were always talking together, French and Germans, as only a small piece of ground separated them. They even called a truce when it was necessary to get water from the fountain in the square of the village. Mon Dieu, but war is stupid! 'You were rehearsing a march with the band,' he continued, 'and the German sentry said it was *très jolie, mais pas ensemble!*' I am sure that sentry became a critic, because he was right. It was not *ensemble*, but it definitely was not *jolie* either!

"At this time my deliverance came from the deplorable band, and from the lamentable war. I had been twenty-six months at the front when my commanding officer received a telegram from the War Office to the effect that the soldat Monteux was to report to Paris immediately. I then learned that a Ballet Russe company was to go to the United States and that Diaghilev had asked for me to be released from duty at the front to accompany them as conductor. You can imagine my joy. I must say, however, the rest of my family were extremely worried. The idea of crossing an ocean full of U-boats seemed a most hazardous undertaking, especially to my poor mother.

"I laugh now when I think of my exodus from the regiment. I was to meet a truck at a village about thirty miles from the place where we were stationed. You can imagine the ludicrous spectacle I made, as I trudged along from village to village past various companies of soldiers, carrying a violin case in one hand, music under my arm, and a gun in the other, with a loaded knapsack on my back. Peasants and soldiers alike poked fun at me: '*Eh bien,* that's a queer way to fight a war!' I assure you, that mileage was the longest I ever made.

"We sailed on the old *Rochambeau* (S. L. Grigorief in his admirable book writes they sailed on the *Lafayette,* but Maestro insists it was the *Rochambeau*), slipping out of the harbor at Bordeaux, lights dimmed and engine muffled. It was a bit nerve-wracking, to say the least. The trip lasted eight days. I remember the black nights and the fact that I spent most of my time eating and sleeping. The food was not copious and not too good, but it was like ambrosia to me, after long months in the army.

"We arrived in New York one bright day in September, 1916. Mr. Otto Kahn met us at the boat with an army of reporters. I must say they were much more interested in the pretty ballet dancers than in the conductor, although the advance notices read, 'With the Ballet as chief conductor will come a conductor high placed in the younger generation of musicians, Pierre Monteux, famed throughout Europe.'

"I went immediately to the home of my friend George Barrère, the great flautist, and awaited word from Nijinsky as to the hour for rehearsal. I was very anxious to meet the orchestra which, of course, I did not know. I need not have worried, as the orchestra was an excellent one, composed of New York musicians. (We call it a pick-up orchestra today.) Frederick Fradkin, a marvelous violinist, was the concert-master. I had no trouble at all with the orchestra, but there was discord all around me. It seemed everyone was in an advanced state of nerves. Nijinsky and Robert Edmond Jones were creating *Till Eulenspiegel* together, a ballet composed on the music

of Richard Strauss, and there were several verbal alterca-
tions between them. At times I had the feeling that their
tense relationship would eventually explode. Nijinsky,
continually irritated because of his lack of skill as a choreographer, insulted the sensitive young American and
heaped typical Russian slurs and indignities on his head.
There was not enough time for rehearsals of this new
ballet, as the dancers arrived late; then Nijinsky strained
a muscle and was immobilized for days.

"I added to his misery by refusing to conduct the work,
as it was by a living German composer, an enemy of
France. I had just left the trenches, I had bitterly experienced the siege of Verdun, I had left my French com-
patriots suffering from the result of long months of a
devastating war, and I simply could not participate in a
project which would send a considerable sum of money to
Germany. And I was too cognizant of the fact that this
country had already declared war on France twice during
my family's lifetime.

"I had long discussions with Nijinsky about my attitude. He would always end up by reiterating that he also
was an enemy of Germany, being a good Russian, but
that he would put on *Till* just the same. I said, 'Do what
you want, but I cannot.' He had not participated in the
war as I had, but had passed his time living in luxury in
beautiful Bar Harbor, Maine, that summer. Otto Kahn
took my part and engaged Anselm Goetzl to conduct the
work in New York and Boston. *Till* was conducted on tour
by the piccolo player of the orchestra. The orchestra was
composed of fifty-five musicians, so of course *Till* was
played with parts missing. It was a queer arrangement of
Strauss's music. This did not bother Nijinsky; for him
the music had secondary place. I never would have con-

ducted *Till* under these circumstances, war or no war. I
conducted everything else. They called me the 'Soldier
Conductor.' I laughed later when America entered the
war, and many orchestras refused to play Beethoven!

"We toured eighteen cities from coast to coast (we
even visited Hollywood and met the new actor, Charlie
Chaplin) and the tour finished in February, 1917, in
Albany, New York. I had been given an extension of
three months by the French Government to finish it. I
was also mentioned in the Chamber of Deputies and
highly praised for my attitude in the Strauss episode. I
remember Boston, New Orleans and San Francisco as
three cities having great character. I little realized I
would one day conduct two of their symphony orchestras.

"I remember the strike of the soloists in the middle of
the tour, due to Nijinsky's having the understudies dance
their roles in what he called 'secondary' towns. I felt his
nerves were at the breaking-point many times. Often I
could hear the dancer and his wife bickering in the
drawing-room next to mine. I assure you, *chérie*, when
Russians argue, they *intend* to be heard!

"And so, another season with the Russian Ballet was
finished for me. Otto Kahn introduced me to the director
of the Metropolitan Opera, Gatti-Casazza, and after an
interview with the great man, I sent a cablegram to
Alfred Cortot, who was employed at the Ministry of War,
in Paris. I told him I had been asked to conduct French
Opera at the 'Met' and desired to stay, if I was not needed
by my country. He cabled back 'ACCEPT,' and the French
Consul in New York, Monsieur Paul Bibili, received the
order to 'demobilize Monteux.' So I stayed on in this
country which has become my own."

III

THE METROPOLITAN OPERA—

THE BOSTON SYMPHONY

Knightsbridge,
London,
September 1962

Caro:

We are happy to be here in our beloved London, where the Maestro is, as you know, the Principal Conductor of the London Symphony Orchestra. He took on these arduous duties two years ago (1960), when he was eighty-six!

Now we are settled in a charming hotel in Knightsbridge, one minute from Hyde Park, where we walk every day by the lovely Serpentine. You know the Maestro's love of birds and his constant worry about them in winter when the ground is white with snow. We save every crumb from our table, augmented with gifts from the hotel dining-room, and armed with bags of bread and cracker crumbs, we make a daily call on the swans, ducks, geese, pigeons and swallows in the ancient park.

Today the mist hung low over the quiet water; there was a cold, damp chill in the air which penetrated our good Scotch wool capes; there were few riders on the bridle path, and all in all, London presented *un morne visage*, even to those who love her as we do. We gave our feathered friends our gifts; they gobbled them up quickly and flew away over the black water to more sheltered coves. People hurried by on their way to shelter also, and with the dank mist enveloping us we returned to our cosy

[101

suite with its warm welcoming grate fire, books, flowers, and music. There was also good talk, as I prevailed on the Maestro to talk of his two years in New York at the Metropolitan Opera House.

"I must first tell you, *chérie*, that the summer before I entered the Met as conductor of the French and Russian repertoire, I conducted the New York Civic Orchestra. This was another of Mr. Otto Kahn's projects, and it was an excellent orchestra. I had pleasure working with them, even though we had to play in the New York Armory, which had terrible acoustics. I think we gave some good concerts, in which I tried to make interesting and varied programs, but the critics had already decided that I was not a symphony conductor, but only a conductor of ballets! The articles were so very bad that my orchestra wrote a protestation which they insisted on sending to the newspapers. They first brought it to me to read, and you can imagine how very touched I was by this mark of appreciation from the New York musicians. I asked them to give me this letter as a gift I would always cherish, and not to think of sending it to the newspapers.

"When I arrived at the Metropolitan Opera House, the critics continued in their disapprobation of me, now saying that I was not an opera conductor, but a symphony and ballet conductor! Mr. Otto Kahn, obviously harassed by these articles which reached their apotheosis in a leading magazine having to do with music and artists in the concert and opera world, then told me, 'Don't worry, Monteux, I will stop this.' I wondered how he could educate a critic, but he did, by taking a five hundred dollar advertisement for me in that music magazine. Would you believe it? The articles stopped!

"Mr. Gatti-Casazza then called me to his office and asked me to make him a list of all the operas I had conducted. I did, and the list filled two pages of typewritten paper. He roared with laughter and sent the whole list to the critics. I found all this extremely disagreeable and assure you my first months in the United States were rather unhappy. All these incidents were augmented by a visit from the *chef de claque* at the Met who insisted on my paying a 'nominal' sum to him and his cohorts, if I wished to have a success. I refused, and of course the house was pretty quiet when I entered the pit.

"Years later my dear brother-in-law, Meyer Davis, suggested I allow him to hire a press agent to promote my interests in America, as he knew of two other conductors who were being 'promoted' by clever agents with success. I told him I would not think of such a thing, and would count on any talent I had to promote me. If that was not sufficient, I would return to France.

"In the fall of 1917 I entered the great opera house as conductor of the French repertoire. I stayed two years, conducting *Carmen*, *Faust*, *Samson et Dalila*, *Marouf*, *Mireille*, *Thaïs*, *Le Coq d'Or*, and a few ballets. These various operas were presented with magnificent artists such as Enrico Caruso, Giovanni Martinelli, Marguerite Matzenauer, Geraldine Farrar, Johanna Gadski, Louise Homer, Léon Rothier and many others who will long remain in my memory. These performances were outstanding musical events.

"I remember Caruso, at our first rehearsal together, arrived ten minutes before the scheduled time. In fact, I never knew him to be late for a rehearsal in the two years I presided over the repertoire that he sang with me. He was extremely respectful and the opposite of 'temperamental.' I knew he was the highest paid lyric artist in the world, and you can imagine my surprise, in the first half hour of rehearsal, to hear him sing every measure of his music absolutely on time. I stopped him and said, 'I beg of you, relax, take your time and interpret the role in comfort. You do not have to be so terribly exact with me on this occasion.' He sighed with relief and answered, 'When I sing with a new Maestro, I always sing exactly on measure, until he tells me I may do otherwise. *Merci beaucoup, Maître.*' We had an extremely happy, courteous relationship. He sang Don José in *Carmen* with me many times. Geraldine Farrar, the beautiful American singer, was our Carmen. This attractive diva sang the role one half tone higher than the original key. When I acquainted Caruso with this fact, knowing he detested singing higher than B flat, I expected fireworks. But no, he called his accompanist, we went to a rehearsal room and after working on the beautiful aria, 'La Fleur' for a few minutes, he sang a glorious B, clear as a bell.

"Farrar, on the other hand, very conscious of her stellar role, was usually a bit late for rehearsals, begged my pardon in her charming way, and always found an excuse, legitimate or otherwise, to leave a bit early. Marguerite Matzenauer was, I think, the finest artist I ever worked with. What a joy it was for me to hear her great golden voice ringing above the orchestra sound. I could relax and be sure of this superb singer, I assure you.

"At that time, Gatti-Casazza was married to the soprano, Frances Alda. One day he called me to his office and told me that we were to present an opera called *Marouf*, a work by the French composer Henri Rabaud, to the American public. I was pleased, as I was familiar with the libretto and knew it to be colorful and charming. I was sure the New York audiences would find pleasure in the music also. Then too I was happy to participate in the presentation of a new French opera. However, Madame Alda rebelled in no uncertain fashion when she realized there was no aria in the whole opera for the Princess, the leading feminine role, which she was to sing. Then there were fireworks which nearly exploded the opera house! What a temper that woman had, whew!

"I suggested to Mr. Gatti that he write Rabaud and ask him to insert an aria. This had been done in many operas, even in the music of very great composers. To my surprise, he refused to do this. Well, I decided to do it anyway, as I really wanted that opera presented that year. I looked through the score and at one point found a lovely line where the composer, by developing a few bars, could concoct an aria for the Princess. Henri Rabaud, upon receiving my letter, was favorable to the idea and wrote an aria of not quite two minutes. The temperamental Madame Alda was pacified for the moment, and we proceeded with scheduled rehearsals in peace. Unhappily, this tale of India, so beautifully staged by the Metropolitan Opera, was not a success with the public and was deleted from the repertoire soon after.

"Mr. Gatti always had an answer for everything that came up. Many of them made me smile, but I must say many of them exasperated me also. For instance, I could never accustom myself to singers with Italo-French accents. To me they were comic and laugh-provoking and at times so completely ludicrous as to ruin the musical phrase. I remember especially one singer, a man with an accent I could not possibly accept and about whom I complained to Mr. Gatti. I asked him, 'Why do you always give me Italians with their ghastly French for the small roles? This one, I assure you, Monsieur le Directeur, is impossible!' Monsieur Gatti stroked his handsome beard, looked at me with a wicked glint in his eye, and said very, very softly, 'But Caro Monteux, this one comes from Toulouse, France!'

"Again, in Boston, I confronted him with what I thought a legitimate complaint that my cast for *Samson et Dalila*, the only opera I was to conduct there, was poor and inadequate. Again he stroked his beard, his eyes opened very wide, and said with pained surprise, 'My God, Maestro, I give you Caruso and you are not happy!' Of course he knew it was not Caruso I complained about, but you see, *chérie*, the star system reigned in those days also, alas!

"Gatti was distant and cold, but very impressive. I liked him. He was efficient and direct. It is good to work with directors with these qualifications. There were several conductors at the Metropolitan Opera at that time. One of my colleagues in particular was known to be extremely severe and difficult. He was always bent on showing his great authority over singers and orchestra, often exploding into violent rages and tantrums. On one of our trips to Philadelphia a group of singers was complaining of this. I knew one tenor in particular to be nervous at times, and I asked him, 'Do you give of your best to this Maestro?' He shook his head and said with great vehemence, 'Oh no, Maestro; if I give seventy-five per cent with you, I can only give twenty-five with him; I am petrified when I have to sing with him!' I said, 'H'm, then what is the use of all that authority?'

"I have often pondered over this. A voice is such a personal thing, generated in a singer's body; it is not a mechanical instrument, as such. Many things affect it, especially nerves and ill health. I think a conductor should be aware of this and as helpful as it is within his powers to be with the singing artist.

"I must also tell you of my first experience with that bugaboo 'status,' so often talked about today. As I lived uptown, I decided I must have an automobile to carry me back and forth to the Opera House, as all my colleagues had. Not having too much money, I bought a shiny Ford touring-car for which I paid the huge sum of three hundred dollars. I was so proud of this, my first car. This pride, I am ashamed to say, did not last long. As I was always early to my rehearsals I was the first to park my car behind the theatre. Then a lady star would arrive in a splendid Locomobile with a chauffeur who invariably parked right behind my little chariot. Next in line came the great Caruso with a magnificent Pierce-Arrow, driven by another class-conscious chauffeur. Mr. Gatti's superb and highly polished vehicle came next, and, by the time all were parked, my shiny black Ford touring-car looked like an insignificant baby-carriage. To this day, I can see myself cranking that Ford, with the various chauffeurs looking on my efforts with supercilious disdain.

"One day, while I was driving down Eighth Avenue, the thing gasped and heaved a deep, long sigh. A small explosion then occurred in its innards and, weary of it all, it stopped. Happily I was near the curbing, so I opened the door, stepped onto the sidewalk, tipped my hat politely to the Ford, and walked away a free man. I never went back for it either, I assure you. You may laugh, but it did not seem amusing at the time.

"There are certain things I remember about my first

year in New York City, especially the gum-chewing passengers in the underground, all in the process of grave
mastication, all jaws champing in rhythm with the wheels
of the train! I was amazed, because they all seemed latent
savages to me. How could civilized people behave like
this?

"While I was still at the Met, Boston was looking for a
conductor for the Boston Symphony Orchestra, and I had
been approached by Mr. Brennan, the manager, offering
me the position. My contract with Mr. Gatti-Casazza was
for three years' duration, and I had no reason to ask permission to leave. I recommended Mr. Henri Rabaud, the
composer of *Marouf*, and they engaged him for the following fall. As it happened, he could not arrive in Boston
until November. He was at that time conductor of the
Opera in Paris, and had commitments there. I was asked
to substitute for him, and accepted, as the Metropolitan
Opera did not need me until November.

"I went to Boston and reorganized the orchestra which
had been badly impaired by the loss of German musicians
expelled because of the war. This was a difficult task, I
assure you. Then I only conducted the remade orchestra
for two weeks, because of a terrific epidemic of influenza
raging in the United States and especially in Boston. The
trustees and powers that reigned in city government decided wisely to close Symphony Hall and all theatres and
meeting-places in the city. I was disappointed and went
back to New York. *C'est la vie!*

"The following spring Henri Rabaud was offered the
directorship of the French National Conservatory in
Paris, and he consequently resigned from the Boston
Symphony, leaving the orchestra again without a leader.
Again Mr. Brennan of Boston came to New York and

offered me the permanent position of Conductor of the Boston Symphony. Mr. Gatti-Casazza very kindly relieved me of my contract, as it was spring, and the end of his season, and I went to Boston the following fall. I remember I was full of pride in my new position as head of one of the oldest and finest orchestras in the United States. Little did I realize the years ahead were to be full of trouble and embarrassment for me, as well as for the trustees of that sacrosanct organization."

This was a long letter from London in fog, wind and rain, *caro*, but bad weather is conducive to conversation and letter writing. My next letter will, of course, concern the five years Monteux spent in New England as conductor of the great orchestra of that city on Massachusetts Bay.

London,
April, 1963

Caro:

It is spring in England and my heart sings, "Come down to Kew in lilac time" the whole day long. Today I begged the Maestro to go a'venturing with me. Now in my estimation the way to go a'venturing in London on a fine spring day is to climb the hazardous steps to the top of a double-decker bus, sit on the very front seat, lord of all one surveys as one rolls along the highways and byways of the great city, stopping only for passengers and red lights. The Maestro has a keen sense of adventure and this day he was enthusiastic at the idea of a journey down to Richmond Park, a stroll in the forest where deer and squirrels abound, and where lovers meander down paths

of verdant green in the soft spring air, oblivious of aught
but themselves.

Our fine red chariot, number 73, of the London Trans-
port System, made its way through Kensington, past the
Victoria and Albert monument, and all the fine stores in
Kensington High Street, straight past Hammersmith and
on to Richmond, our destination. We swept around corners with measured speed, felt young and blithesome, completely forgetting our years of life, and simply revelled in
the lovely absurdity of it all. After a fine walk in the park
and a cup of tea complete with sugar, milk, and a bun
(which neither of us takes ordinarily) we climbed
again the dashing red bus and rode it all the way to
Islington, quite the other side of London town; then back
to Knightsbridge weary and hungry for a delicious dinner ordered by Luigi, our more than competent maître
d'hôtel. What does spring do to one, caro?

I do not know why this day made me think of Boston,
unless it is because I have always found a certain British-
ness in that city so dear to my heart. It was there, you
know, that I met the Maestro, and it was there that I received most of my education. I have always found it gay
and yet reserved, and no matter how modern it may aim
to be, I think it will always have a slight Victorian atmosphere. And so, caro mio, as I was thinking of Boston
I asked my dinner companion a few questions relating to
his *séjour* in Symphony Hall on Huntington Avenue of
that city. This is what he told me that evening in London:

"It is difficult for me to think of my five years in Boston without a slight feeling of . . . *amertume*. You
must remember that the predilection of the public, due to
the preference in music of my predecessors, was almost
wholly for the German repertoire. I consequently found

what seemed to me an extremely restricted outlook in music. That great gentleman, father of the Boston Symphony Orchestra, Major Henry L. Higginson, loved everything Germanic. I am sure the war was a terrible shock to him, one that proved fatal, for he died on November 14th, 1919 during my tenure with the orchestra he so loved. He was always perfectly charming to me, but I had the feeling our tastes in music were not completely compatible.

"Mr. W. H. Brennan, the manager, was definitely pro-German and showed it in many ways. I remember one incident which happened directly after the war. I knew Mr. Bruno Walter was coming to America and I suggested we invite him as guest conductor for the Boston Symphony Concerts. This we subsequently did. Well, *chérie*, you would have laughed to see the princely service given my colleague by our manager! I assure you, I was hardly noticed during those two weeks and I wondered at times *who* was conductor of the Boston Symphony Orchestra.

"Once on tour in New York we had the Russian composer-pianist, Sergei Rachmaninoff, as soloist. I was having luncheon at the Biltmore Hotel. At one moment Mr. Brennan came to my table and whispered, 'Mr. Rachmaninoff says you have given him the finest accompaniment he has ever experienced!' I said, 'In that case, why whisper it; why not shout it? After all, I am your conductor!' He looked very surprised by this riposte. Oh, we were always extremely polite and cordial to each other, but I felt our cordiality had no real depth. On the other hand, Mr. George Judd, assistant manager, whom I grew to know and love in later years, was always kind and thoughtful, a true New England gentleman.

"I decided I would broaden the musical outlook of the orchestra, and give the Boston public an idea of music composed in their epoch. This innovation was enthusiastically received by young listeners from the New England Conservatory of Music and the students from the various colleges and universities in that part of Massachusetts. I am not sure the old-timers quite approved of some of the music we played for them. I insisted on including as many American composers as was possible during each season. By so doing, many fine composers, now neglected, such as Foote, Gilbert, Chadwick, Loeffler, Griffes, Converse, Skilton and many other native composers were introduced. I played all works of British composers of that period as well as many French and Italian. It is a very lengthy list I would have to give you, if I were to enumerate the compositions I presented for the first time in Boston.

"I am happy to say my two successors continued this policy. The Boston Symphony Orchestra stands today a modern institution, aware of its duty to the composer of the twentieth century and its paramount position in music education.

"I was in Boston only one year, when the orchestra was literally torn apart by argument and strife. In 1919 there were rumors that many of the musicians in the orchestra favored entering the Musicians' Union. I paid no attention to these rumors at first, as I knew the trustees would never hear of the Boston Symphony Orchestra becoming unionized. However, the attitude of certain members became very disagreeable and unpleasant, and I had difficulty in keeping a semblance of discipline conducive to work. At last a stormy meeting was held and to the astonishment and chagrin of the trustees and myself, forty-five left to join the union. Later many of these musicians went to the Detroit Symphony Orchestra, which Ossip Gabrilowitsch was forming at that time.

"Once again it was my turn to rebuild the orchestra. Happily the musicians I had engaged after the war episode, many of them from the French *fanfare* or band that had toured America during the last period of the war, and who later became the stars of the ensemble, (such as the wonderful English horn player, Louis Speyer, Paul Mimart, G. Mager and others) remained. I gave auditions day after day and recruited a few fine players from the various theatre and restaurant orchestras in Boston and New York. In those halcyon days for the musician, restaurants had very good ensembles playing for the diners. There was no such thing as 'piped-in music,' I assure you. I have always found this 'piped-in music' extremely annoying, and do not appreciate the idea of music from which there is no escape! It is really a form of dictatorship!

"As many of the new players were string players (violins, violas, 'celli and basses) it was necessary to have many rehearsals of these sections alone. Many had never played symphonic music. I was greatly aided in this by Mr. J. Theodorowicz, who had replaced Mr. Frederick Fradkin, the former concertmaster. This was a worrisome and unhappy time, as I went on tour with fifty-five musicians! For our New York concert I concocted a program consisting of the "New World" Symphony of Dvorak, the *Lohengrin* Prelude and Forest Murmurs of Wagner, the *Petite Suite* of Debussy, and the Hungarian March of Berlioz! The public understood our embarrassment and we carried the whole predicament off with flying colors.

"The following spring I went to Paris and advertised for a concertmaster. One day a young man arrived from Finland. He was Russian. I listened to him play for five minutes, no more. He was astonished when I said to him, 'You are the new concertmaster of the Boston Symphony Orchestra.' We shook hands, I said, '*À très bientôt à Boston.*' He arrived in the fall of 1920 and has been there ever since! His name is Richard Burgin. He is a wonderful musician-violinist, and in these later years has become a very fine conductor. I was very fortunate in my choice of Burgin. My trust in him, and a score of others I engaged, never wavered. We worked very hard to return the ensemble to its former glory and, at last, after four years of patient music-making, my pleasure and pride in my orchestra was intense."

Philip Hale, the Boston music critic, wrote in 1924: "Monteux formed and molded the orchestra in the face of obstacles that would have daunted a man of less patience, courage, and artistic enthusiasm. He had skill and taste as an interpreter of ancient, modern, and ultramodern music." That was only a year, Caro, before the strange development he then described:

"I did not have long to enjoy the fruit of my efforts, however, because I was told it was the 'policy' of the Boston Symphony to change conductors every five years. I was replaced by Serge Koussevitsky, a Russian, conducting orchestras at that time in London and Paris.

"It is the custom here in the United States to make an intensive *réclame* for the forthcoming conductor in the last year of the incumbent. Perhaps this is necessary, but I do not think the trustees of orchestras realize how very embarrassing and grievous, not to say vexatious, this policy (when carried out in the efficient manner of American managers) can be to a sensitive musician. In my case, I felt deeply my last year in Boston as a sort of interim between the known and the unknown.

"I was told by Judge Frederick P. Cabot, in a charming speech made at a reception in Symphony Hall just before the season's end, 'This is not goodbye; you will come back to *your* orchestra many times.' I left Boston in the month of May, 1925, and did not return for twenty-six years! Strangely enough, the five year policy existed no longer."

He sighed deeply, and I changed the subject by asking him what he considered among his most enjoyable experiences in Boston.

"During the 1923 season the President of the Board of Trustees (Judge Cabot) asked me if I would care to hear a young tenor he thought had 'immense promise.' I replied that I would be delighted, and accordingly went with him one afternoon to a fine Boston home for—eh, tea.

"The artist was Roland Hayes, Negro tenor, who at that time had garnered huge successes in Europe, singing for royalty and sophisticated audiences in many of the capitals there. I was simply enchanted with Mr. Hayes' voice, his erudition in matters pertaining to music and his charming manners. His wonderful warm personality imbued everything he sang. I was so enthusiastic after the lovely recital that I said, 'He must sing with the orchestra in Symphony Hall. He is an American, and I want him.'

"Mr. William Brennan, as usual, found many reasons why this would be quite impossible. 'Oh Mr. Monteux, the hall would be full of Negroes, we could not have this.' I finally made it clear that this excuse was false, as the hall was fully subscribed by white Bostonians. The manager's hesitation seemed strange to a Frenchman; we have no squeamish fastidiousness as to the pigment of a man's skin, be it yellow, black, or white. As a matter of fact, there are few really white people as such; most are different shades of red or pink, some even purple, ha ha!

"Mr. Brennan persisted, however, and in the end suggested a special concert in which to present Mr. Hayes to the audiences of Boston. I said, 'Then the hall WOULD be full of Negroes.' Well, at last, after much discussion, we decided that Roland Hayes would be engaged as soloist at the regular Friday afternoon concert of November sixteenth of that year.

"This was undoubtedly the first time a Negro had ever sung or appeared as soloist in any form with a symphony orchestra in the United States. I am very proud of this achievement. I think it was one of my happiest experiences while in Boston. Roland Hayes later sang with me in Paris, with the Concertgebouw Orchestra in Amsterdam, and with my orchestra in San Francisco. At this pair of concerts in Boston, looking every inch an aristocratic gentleman and singing in a most aristocratic manner, elegantly musical, 'Un aura amorosa' from the opera *Cosi Fan Tutte* of Mozart and the aria, 'The Repose of the Holy Family,' from *L'Enfance du Christ* of Hector Berlioz, he lived up to all my faith and confidence in him, faith in his future and confidence in his immense artistry, which I was sure would sweep him on to success in this, his country. Country where his own grandmother had been a slave! I insisted he sing two Negro spirituals, *Bye and Bye*, and *Go Down Moses*, that stirring command to old Pharoah to 'let my people go!' The result was instantaneous success with public and critics alike.

Pierre Monteux, second from left, as a young man in the 1890's with a group of convivial friends at Etretat.

Edward Grieg, the composer, seated in the foreground with the Johannes Wolf Quartet in May, 1903. Monteux is second from right.

Camille Saint-Saëns, at the piano, in his last concert (1913) conducted by Monteux (*far left*) at the Salle Gaveau, Paris.

On tour in the U.S. with the Ballet Russe, the troupe visited Charlie Chaplin's studio during the filming of *Easy Street* (1916). Monteux is in second row center, with Nijinsky and Chaplin to his left.

Monteux as conductor of the Boston Symphony Orchestra.

THE FAREWELL SEASON OF PIERRE MONTEUX

❦ ❦

Pierre Monteux will complete this season his five-year period as conductor of the Boston Symphony Orchestra, and will then return to France.

Mr. Monteux came to an orchestra which for many years had set the standard of ultimate perfection in symphonic performance. In the four seasons past, his breadth of vision has given a new quality to the Boston Symphony concerts, and his tireless hand has wrought new beauties of tone and ensemble. Last season he was praised on every hand for having splendidly realized ambitions of executive precision and eloquence which add another mark of artistic achievement to the record of the Orchestra.

Pierre Monteux is setting a precedent in the Boston Symphony Concerts and the symphony concerts of America which will never be forgotten. His programmes are unexampled in freedom from routine, in keen espousal of every national school, and in discriminate championship of the newer music still to be recognized.

This may be America's last opportunity to hear Pierre Monteux, the greatest of French conductors. From every indication, he will be heard under ideal conditions. He has numerous scores of special interest to put upon his programmes, and he has an organization of supreme qualities ready to give this music performance. The season should be one of the finest in the annals of the Orchestra.

The program announcement of Monteux's farewell season in Boston.

Top: At the organ, his favorite pastime.

Center: Studying a score.

Bottom: In Amsterdam with the "Friends" of the Concertgebouw Orchestra.

With two young pupils at the Domaine School for Conductors.

His 75th birthday party in San Francisco, 1950. From the left, Madame Monteux, Admiral Chester Nimitz, Mrs. Sigismund Stern, and Monteux.

Above: The Monteuxs with Mrs. Meyer Davis.

Opposite: At Hancock, Maine. The flag-raiser is Monteux's father-in-law, Eugene Hamilton Hodgkins.

Opposite: As honorary fire chief in Hancock, Maine and as an honorary member of the London Fire Brigade.

With the Mayor of Montreal, on Monteux's 80th birthday (1955).

Photo by Eric Auerbach

Conducting the London Symphony Orchestra in rehearsal, 1963.

Entering the Frederick Mann auditorium in Tel Aviv with Abe Cohen of the Israeli Philharmonic (right), Niels Gron (left), and Madame Monteux.

The last portrait, taken by Eric Auerbach.

"This concert most certainly paved the way for the great Negro contraltos Marian Anderson, Grace Bumbry, sopranos Dorothy Maynor, Mattawilda Dobbs, Leontyne Price, bass Paul Robeson and many other great Negro artists who have graced and enobled our concert platforms since that momentous Friday in November, 1923." (Caro, I believe Mr. William Brennan managed Mr. Roland Hayes after the singer had proved to the doubtful man his supreme artistry!)

"A few years ago, if you remember, *chérie*, we were invited to visit Mr. and Mrs. Hayes, and their lovely and intelligent daughter in their charming home in Brookline, Massachusetts. I will never forget how terribly touched I was when we all bowed our heads for grace before luncheon, and the delight I felt when the Hayes family sang in beautiful three-part harmony our petition to God to bless our food. Wherever and whenever we meet, I have always experienced a feeling of deep affection for this marvelous man.

"It has always been the custom of the Boston Symphony Orchestra to give a few concerts in our country's capital every season. I was very proud, as a Frenchman, to have been chosen to head this fine ensemble, and especially to present it to the Washington audiences. I knew that the German Ambassador and his staff usually attended the concerts of my predecessor, Dr. Karl Muck, and that many formal and informal dinners and supper parties had been given in his honor by his excellency the representative of Deutschland in America. I supposed, and hoped, that the same procedure would take place when I visited Washington with the orchestra, and that I would be received by the French Ambassador, Jules Jusserand, with perhaps a show of pride on his part.

"Armed with my card, I therefore presented myself the first day of my first visit to the capital at the door of the French Embassy. I was received by an attendant and given a seat in a reception room, where I waited what seemed to me an interminable time. At last he reappeared and announced that his Excellency the Ambassador could not see me. He was at luncheon. This I did not believe, as it was long after three o'clock. There were no regrets expressed by attendant or Ambassador. I must say I had no regrets later either, as the French Ambassador never attended one of my concerts in the five years of my visits to Washington with the Boston Symphony Orchestra. On the other hand, the German Ambassador and his whole staff attended *all* of the concerts and were most enthusiastic and complimentary. I am forced to admit that this attitude on the part of France's representatives in many countries I have visited during seventy-five years as an artist, playing my instrument or conducting orchestras, is usual. I have been very often both vexed and hurt by it, not only for myself but for the societies I represented. I realize only too well, in the instance of Washington, that one Ambassador loved music and the other evidently loved *la cuisine francaise* and his stomach!

"On one occasion in Washington I had Sergei Rachmaninoff as soloist. As we had one evening free, someone suggested we go to the theatre to hear an extraordinary ensemble called the Six Brown Brothers, experts on the saxophone. The theatre was full and in our places in a box we were entertained and amused by the show. At last the long-awaited Brown Brothers appeared and played with astounding virtuosity a medley of popular tunes. Then, with deep bows in the direction of our box, they proceeded to play, in jazz form, the famous Prelude by Rachmaninoff. I have never seen anyone quite so angry. The composer, beside himself with rage, stomped out of the box, exclaiming, 'They have no respect for anything in this country, no respect, no respect!' I tried to calm him, explaining it was their idea of a compliment, as jazz was their medium of expression. To no avail; he simply could not understand!

"I have to smile when I think of the occasion Fritz Kreisler, wanting to improve my English, no doubt, invited me to the theatre in Washington on another free night to hear a famous actor and a wonderful company playing in Shakespeare's *Hamlet*. If my memory serves me right, I think it was Mr. Walter Hampden who played Hamlet, and whom later I admired very much in many plays. On this occasion, in spite of Kreisler's assuring me that I would understand every word ('the English would be so very perfect and so very beautiful'), I truly suffered for three hours or more, as I did not understand one word of what was said on the stage. I have always had difficulty reading Shakespeare, due to the form of the sentences and the old English idioms, but I persevered and came to love *Romeo and Juliet*, *King Lear*, *The Merchant of Venice* and other wonderful plays. I enjoyed conducting years ago, for the Société Wagner in Amsterdam, Verdi's *Falstaff*, which is based on *The Merry Wives of Windsor*, as you well know.

"Oh, there were many things occurring during the five seasons I conducted the Boston Symphony Orchestra that hurt me, and I cannot say that I was happy in this post. Proud, yes; contented artistically, no. Twenty-six years later when Mr. Henry Cabot, the new President of the Board of Trustees wrote and invited me to return, I hesitated, but a second letter, touching and cordial, seconded

by a beautiful letter from my dear colleague, Charles
Munch, decided me. I returned to a warm welcome from
the management and the Boston public. I have made
many tours with the orchestra in the past years, notably
one American tour and two European tours, one of which
took us to Soviet Russia. Mr. George Judd is no more in
Boston as manager, but Mr. Thomas Perry is there and I
feel genuine cordiality extended toward me whenever I
am at Symphony Hall or in Tanglewood.

"*Chérie*, I am one who needs to feel appreciated and
loved—as I am in Holland and England—to really ex-
pand and give of myself. This feeling is human and I
know every artist feels as I do. Music simply cannot
breathe in an atmosphere of contention."

And so, Caro, here ends all he said of the Boston episode. I hope to write you again from London of his return
to Paris during the 1924 season there.

London
September, 1963

Caro:

I have been in a state of enchantment and geniality
for seven wonderful days, due to two octogenerians and
their wise and most precious maturity, manifested in
many ways. I'm sure you have guessed the first gentleman was our Maestro. The second was Don Pablo Casals,
most fabled 'cellist of this century. You cannot imagine,
Caro, the spell the very presence of this tiny man of
eighty-seven casts over all who have the privilege of
knowing him—it is extraordinary!

The first concerts of the Royal Jubilee Season of the

London Symphony Orchestra (Maestro's orchestra) took place this week also. The soloists appearing with him were Mr. Isaac Stern, the prodigious violinist, and Mr. Leonard Rose, marvelous 'cellist. Accompanying them was the third member of their famous trio, the noted pianist, Mr. Eugene Istomin, who, though not playing with the orchestra, was notably in evidence.

Johannes Brahms' double concerto for violin and 'cello present the violinist and 'cellist together. The violin concerto of the Finnish composer, Jean Sibelius, and Richard Strauss' *Don Quixote* gave each the opportunity to bedazzle the public of the huge Festival Hall, where the concerts are given each week of the concert season. This great auditorium, filled with enthusiastic London music-lovers, standing tier on tier in honor of a famous artist, is a sight never to be forgotten. Ignored is the unesthetic interior, the murky, dull brown walls, the fantastic boxes or loges jutting out into the theatre, for all the world like giant cash registers, the truly questionable architecture of the interior as a whole, and one is swept off one's feet by mass response to glorious music played by superb musicians. This was a week, Caro, of jubilant appreciation.

During one of the rehearsals the three artists conceived the idea of a surprise dinner for Don Pablo, who had arrived three days before. It appeared he had asked incessantly to see his old friend Monteux, with whom he had been in correspondence, and was told that Monteux was very much occupied with rehearsals but would undoubtedly call him on the telephone.

It was arranged secretly, however, that the trio invite Casals and his lovely, dark-eyed young wife, Marta, for a dinner at the Westbury Hotel. The invitation was accepted, but no mention was made of Monteux. Accordingly on the propitious happy evening he and his wife arrived at the private dining-room and sat at a table that had been beautifully decorated with flaming red roses and red candles by Madame Vera Stern, Isaac Stern's charming and very efficient wife.

Don Pablo was delighted with the festive board which he thought 'had a real Spanish air' and after a pause in which he made a little speech of greeting and thanks, sat down, looked around appreciatively, then remarked with surprise, "But the table lacks three guests; who will sit in the empty places?"

He was told Leonard Rose was coming, but would be a bit late. As for the other guests, "The extra places were certainly an error on the part of the management of the hotel!" He was satisfied with this explanation, and nothing more was said.

To amuse and distract the master, they presented him with an old program dating long before the last war. It interested and intrigued him immensely, as it contained pictures of Alfred Cortot, French pianist; Jacques Thibaud, violinist; and Pablo Casals, 'cellist and presented a concert of trios given in the Salle Pleyel by these famous artists beloved of Paris. He laughed heartily at the pictures, exclaiming, *"Mon Dieu,* thirty years, we were young and beau then, *n'est-ce pas?"*

(I well remember that concert, Caro. I was there in a box in the middle of the auditorium. It was a gala event, I assure you, as each artist had his bevy of admirers. Alfred Cortot sat at the concert-grand Pleyel piano, a withdrawn, languid, ghostlike figure, completely occupied with his own part in the ensemble. In spite of this intense occupation with self, he succeeded in dropping a few precious notes and playing a few wrong ones from time to time, quite oblivious to its effect on the music being played, or on the unity demanded in chamber music. The elegant Jacques Thibaud, chic and engaging personality, stood at least eight feet away, alone, and charmingly engrossed in the lovely silken tones he produced from his famous Stradivarius violin, oblivious also to their effect in the ensemble. Last, but most certainly not least, there to the left, chair pulled to the extreme edge of the stage, his head turned as if in disdain away from his 'cello and from his partners of the trio, sat the great Casals, also oblivious to anything other than his own superb music-making which absorbed him completely. Trio? No; but a magnificent, fascinating spectacle of self-devotion. Yes! I must say, we all enjoyed the concert.

Five minutes after Big Ben had tolled forth eight o'clock, we arrived at the Westbury Hotel. Leonard Rose was awaiting us and escorted us immediately to the private dining-room. We entered inconspicuously by a side door, directly behind Casals, who was occupied in looking at and discussing the old program. He did not see us enter, of course, and was quite unaware of our presence 'til Maestro, who was standing in back of him, tapped Don Pablo's shoulder a right smart tap. The master looked up in surprise, gave a great shout, jumped up, and the two old friends fell into each other's arms. They hugged and kissed on both cheeks many times, a few happy tears were shed, and the guests also had very tight throats, so contagious was the emotion generated by these two ardent comrades of bygone days.

Dear friend, you should have heard the pithy conversation of these two Maestros. Monteux, eighty-eight years old, very up-to-date in his dark serge suit, blue tie with red and white stripes, pearl tie pin, his red rosette of a Commander of the Legion of Honor; Casals, dressed much more sedately, all blacks and grays, a lovable, quaint figure and old friend. There was talk of happenings fifty years ago, when both were young and life, full of possibilities, stretched before them; talk of the great performers of that epoch, and their various techniques which, they both agreed, had no relation whatsoever to the extraordinary technical proficiency of today's performing artist. They voiced their conviction that musical demonstration in those days had deeper meaning and intensity because in many cases knowledge of and acquaintance with the composer was literally part and parcel of life. For example, Edouard Colonne knew Hector Berlioz. Pablo Casals knew Saint-Saëns, Joachim, Brahms and many others. They agreed that the copying of master-recordings by young artists, so prevalent at this time, is very harmful. They were thankful for the days when the young aspiring musician did his own thinking about music and by his own endeavors grew to know the master composers whose works he played. Even if the results were at times questionable, the listener was profoundly moved by the intensity of personality.

Then came talk of Paris and of Parisians of that epoch, the early years of the twentieth century. Saint-Saëns, Debussy, César Franck, Ravel, Pierné and many others. Saint-Saëns, they both agreed, was not only a colossal musician, but a composer sadly neglected today. It is true that he was frequently sarcastic and at times extremely disagreeable, but nevertheless he really "knew his business" and one must admire the formidable musician he was. They spoke of the "wishy-washy" and puerile way the works of Debussy are played today. Maestro said, "The great Claude often stood behind me as I rehearsed one of his works and literally shouted, 'Monteux, that's a *forte*, and when I write a *forte*, I want a *forte!*' He played the piano realistically and I might say uncompromisingly, to say the least, when he played his scores for me. Every indication was followed meticulously. Oh no! Debussy was decidedly not a wishy-washy personality. Of course most composers when playing their orchestral score on a piano are apt to exaggerate and play too loudly. They hear the full orchestra as they have written it, and the poor piano is the innocent martyr to their ardent enthusiasm. Debussy was quite the contrary; he knew exactly what he wanted to hear and how it should sound, and I never remember him losing himself in ardent enthusiasm or forgetting what he was after."

Casals nodded in agreement as to Debussy's way of playing and thinking; then they both discarded Pierné with eloquent shrugs, evidently having no appreciation for the man or his music. Indeed, Casals was the hero of a famous law suit because of Pierné's "insult to the Dvorak Concerto for 'Cello," Don Pablo's choice for one of the Colonne Orchestra concerts of which Pierné was conductor, and for which he had been engaged. It seems Gabriel Pierné had the temerity and poor taste to call this beautiful concerto by Anton Dvorak "dirty music." On hearing this remark, Casals withdrew, refusing absolutely to play with a man who considered the music he was accompanying "dirty"! As he had a signed contract to play this concert, he lost the suit! Maestro then remarked, and Leonard Rose smiled delightedly, "The adagio of the Dvorak 'Cello Concerto is one of the most beautiful slow movements ever written. You were quite right in your refusal, *cher ami*."

After a while, I heard Casals say with vehemence that the modern composer's music could not last, as it is soulless and lacking in melody! (Indeed, Maestro has a magnificent letter from him written from Puerto Rico to this effect.) Monteux remarked that the modern is a product of the age in which he exists, that is, a scientific and mechanical century. Since scientific and mechanical production becomes obsolete soon after its introduction, it is his opinion that much modern music conceived and composed by today's composer will no doubt have the same destiny.

Later in the week we listened to Casals' oratorio which he, with profound, fervent sincerity, composed as an incentive toward peace in this world. It is called *The Manger*, and tells of the glorious and mysterious birth night of Jesus Christ. I realized while listening to the rather old-fashioned and at times curiously naive music, played beautifully by the London Philharmonic Orchestra and conducted by Don Pablo himself, the natural antipathy he must feel for modern harmonic construction.

I felt, Caro, this man's great age, agile and enthusiastic though he is. I could not help but compare him with our Maestro, who at the moment is deep in the works of Hindemith, Britten and Bliss, and who has learned many modern works since his eightieth year. I was very proud of him that week as he and Leonard Rose gave a "spellbinding" performance of Richard Strauss's *Don Quixote* before a delirious Festival Hall public which filled every seat in the vast auditorium.

We return to Paris in my next letter, and have an exciting reunion with Diaghilev in the spring of 1924; the spring of Igor Stravinsky and *Les Noces* at the Champs Elysées Theatre.

IV

RETURN TO EUROPE:

THE CONCERTGEBOUW

Caro, mio amico:

The wind was blowing out of the west, the leaves were falling in Green Park and we treaded paths of gold and copper. Fat pigeons followed us, heads bobbing incessantly like topheavy waddling old ladies. The autumn sun shone through an enchanting haze, lending a Corot air to the scene before us. After our stroll, we sat on a wooden bench to rest and partake of the sun's faint rays, a rare luxury in London this autumn of 1963, I assure you.

After a few minutes of desultory conversation, I said to the Maestro, "Do tell me of that spring in Paris after leaving Boston. Were you happy to return to your native France after years in the United States?" I waited a few minutes, as he seemed in no mood for reminiscence. Then he looked at me and, with a sad smile, answered my rather abrupt question:

"No, I was not happy to return to France. I have never been happy to return to Paris. I was happy the first twenty years of my life in Paris; but ever since, I have experienced nothing but sad frustration every time I have returned to conduct concerts with a French orchestra. In 1924 I returned after conducting for two years the fine orchestra at the Metropolitan Opera House and for five years one of the world's greatest ensembles, the Boston

Symphony Orchestra, which by my own efforts I had
built into a magnificent musical instrument, disciplined
and proud of its achievement. I knew, even if I were
offered an orchestra in my native city, which was doubtful, as all had their own permanent conductors, I would
find none of the attributes absolutely necessary to a first-
class ensemble.

"After a week or so in the capitol, spent visiting my
mother and father and the rest of my numerous family
[his father died immediately after his return], I received
offers of concerts in London, Manchester, Liverpool,
Stockholm, Oslo and Bergen, Norway. These engagements pleased me very much, but they were not cities
where I would be offered a permanent post. Even at that
time the great orchestras of every European city were
conducted by talented native conductors and the foreign
musician, composer and conductor were invited guests.
Therefore, you can understand, I was worried as to my
future.

"One day I was in a taxi, in the middle of an army
of automobiles on the Champs Elysées wondering if we
would ever advance, so impossible was the traffic. Then
to my utter astonishment I heard a familiar voice shouting, 'Monteux, Monteux, wait, wait, I must speak with
you!' It was Diaghilev.

"Our drivers drew up to the curbing, Diaghilev entered my taxi, gave a seemingly great sigh of relief,
hugged and kissed me and said, 'Dieu merci, you are
just the person I have been looking for since yesterday
noon.' I was completely nonplussed and said, 'But why?'

" 'You are not aware that I am going to have a season of
ballet at the Champs Elysées Theatre in June, a Russian-
French season?' I answered that I had just returned from

America and that ballet was at that moment far from my thoughts. 'Well,' said he, 'André Messager is to conduct my French répertoire, and you, mon cher Monteux, must conduct the Russian ballets.'

"I explained that I was extremely tired from having conducted a long season of concerts in Boston and on tour, and that I hoped to go to Dieppe for a rest. 'Impossible, impossible, mon cher Monteux, you have never let me down before, and I absolutely count on you this time, *je vous en prie*, don't say no!'

"As usual and as always he won out, and I found myself, a week after, rehearsing another season of ballet at the Champs-Elysées Theatre with the Ballets Sergei Diaghilev, in June of 1924. The name became Ballet Russe de Monte Carlo somewhat later.

"The *pièce de résistance* of that short season was undoubtedly the ballet *Les Noces*, which had been performed the previous year. This ballet on a peasant wedding theme by Igor Stravinsky was scored for four pianos, a few percussion instruments, Russian chorus and two soloists. For some strange reason Diaghilev was very enthusiastic about this music and the ballet. Stravinsky had given him two successes with *Petrouchka* and *Le Sacre du Printemps*, and I think he counted on *Les Noces* to complete the trio. He was not far from right, because when it had been presented at the Gaîté Lyrique Theatre on July 13, 1923, it had a very legitimate success, comparable to many of previous years. The choreography was by Bronislava Nijinska, sister af Vaslav. It was excellent— so good in fact that thereafter she was called La Nijinska! The music made one think of archaic Russia; I found it deeply moving. Nijinska had employed iconic gestures and primitive movement in her choreography which nobly suited the music.

"All this I did not know, of course, that first day of rehearsals at the Champs Elysées. Stravinsky was to conduct the first presentation of *Les Noces* and I was delegated, as conductor of the Russian repertoire, to conduct all others. I sat in the stalls with my score at the first rehearsal, following every note. I had studied it thoroughly and I at once noticed that no one came in on time, chorus or soloists. (Stravinsky at that time was not the conductor he is today, having little or no experience with ensembles.) The performance went through, and was a huge success with the Paris public, who always adored Stravinsky. That evening I met Diaghilev in one of the foyers and asked him when I could have a rehearsal of *Les Noces*. He looked cross, and literally yelled at me, 'Rehearsal, what? Mais mon cher Monteux, the composer just conducted it!'

"I answered, 'The composer can do what he wants with his work but I have to play what is written. It will cost nearly nothing, there is no orchestra.'

"This last idea pleased him and after a pause in which I knew he was figuring just what it would cost, he said, 'All right, you can have the chorus tomorrow night, and the soloists the next day.'

"I worked with the chorus, who knew their parts perfectly; it sufficed to give them their cues at the right places. As for the soloists, they sang in any key and anywhere. They had to learn their parts. A few days after that rehearsal, I had my first performance of *Les Noces*. It went perfectly and I was satisfied, but it had not the success as when conducted by the composer. *C'est la vie!* Ha ha!

"I left immediately after this season of ballets and went to Dieppe, where I passed the summer, returning to Paris in the fall."

In my next letter, *caro*, we leave dancers forever more, and enter the truly splendid epoch of the Maestro's career. Au revoir 'til Amsterdam, where I shall meet you in the famous *soloistenkamer* of the Concertgebouw.

Amsterdam, Holland,
November, 1963

Caro:

In Holland this is the month of mobile black and gray clouds, pelting rain, and cold penetrating wind from the North Sea. The bare branches of the great trees along the canal show their twisted reflections in the dark water. I'm sure this must seem to you (used as you are these past months to sunny Rome) cheerless and depressing. Perhaps we are very queer or perhaps we do not need sunshine for happiness, because we are always happy here in the Netherlands. The reason? Dutch interiors are notably colorful and furnished with warmth and intimacy. One is ever aware of the past, in the form of decoration, no matter how old or modern the house or the apartment. The interiors of Vermeer are suggested, and the reds and golds of Franz Hals and the rich tones of Rembrandt. These interiors please us immensely. As we have lived in them on and off for forty years, we feel snug, comfortable and contented. The north wind may roar and the rain descend in torrents, but the Monteuxs are extremely satisfied with life in old Amsterdam.

For the Maestro, of course, one of the real reasons for elation is always the return to that noble and imposing

edifice, the Concertgebouw, which is the home of the
Concertgebouw Orchestra. It is a fine sight at night to
stand in the center of the *plein* (a long stretch of green-
sward lined with trees) with the castle-like Rijks Museum
floodlighted at one end, and the gray stone Victorian
Concert Hall at the other, the short frontal columns aglow
in the white light. On the topmost peak is the lovely lyre
we have all grown to cherish, shining like a jewel in the
dark of the night, an affirmation that this building is
indeed the home of music.

As usual, we have many young men from Maestro's
school in Maine here with us, and we are a small troupe
following our leader as we ascend the red-carpeted stairs.
The Maestro counts the stairs each time, and has counted
them every day beginning forty years ago, when he first
climbed them to the conductor's room and the *soloistenkamer*. All the student-conductors are excited at the
thought of hearing the wonderful orchestra conducted by
their master in rehearsal.

I have never once in these late years entered the old
soloistenkamer without saying to Maestro, "For me, this
place is haunted!" He laughs, but one day he admitted
that he also feels the indelible past pervading the old
building. Of course there is the great Willem Mengelberg
whose spirit, I am sure, has never left these halls and
corridors he so loved, since his lonely death in the snowy
solitude of a Swiss valley. In a never-ending line, I feel
the presences of the magnificent artists and composers
whose music has filled the great hall over the years. If
one listens, one hears (if one is so privileged) a glorious,
yes, even a rollicking *Te Deum!*

I am sure you will agree with me, *caro,* that one cannot write of the Concertgebouw and music in Holland

without the name of Willem Mengelberg occurring time and time again, because, when all is said and done, it was truly Mengelberg's tenacious, dominating will and talent which eventually gave the Concertgebouw in Amsterdam its tremendous prestige in the world of music. I think he was one of the most fascinating personalities I have ever met. He was at the same time kind and generous, unkind and small, bombastic yet gentle, childishly naive, foolishly proud and pompous, yet ridden with a feeling of unworthiness, religious yet at times positively hedonistic. He entertained like a prince. Truly, a more complex character never lived!

We were a part of the life in the Concertgebouw for ten long years, in the building which was in effect the musical home of Willem Mengelberg. Many have asked how we managed to "get along" with this so-called terror of the orchestra world. I can answer truthfully and very simply that, in all those years, there was no question of "getting along." There was never a word of disagreement between the two colleagues who led the great Dutch orchestra through that decade together. Many will say, "Of course, Mengelberg was the boss." This is far from the truth. He often told Maestro to change any musicians he saw fit, as he had perfect faith and confidence in his ability to make orchestras. The Boston episode proved it, if an example were needed. This trust gave Pierre the opportunity to change a few of the musicians during those years for the good of the ensemble.

I remember the second week we were in Holland. That was in 1924. Pierre conducted *Le Sacre du Printemps* of Igor Stravinsky. The orchestra, as well as the Dutch public, found it as strange and upsetting as had the public in Paris many years before. After twelve strenuous rehearsals the concerts were given and there was great excitement throughout the Netherlands. As usual, many hated the work and as many were thrilled by it. This was true of the orchestra as well as the public.

The following week, Mengelberg came to Pierre's first rehearsal and asked if he could speak to the orchestra. Maestro said, "Of course," wondering at the same time what the Dutch conductor was going to say. As he could not understand a word of the language, he was rather worried. Mengelberg strode to the podium and talked earnestly to the ensemble. Pierre heard the words "music," "Stravinsky" and "Monteux." When the speech was finished, this supposedly spoiled tyrant came to Pierre, and with his arm over the Frenchman's shoulder, led the orchestra in cheers for his guest from *la belle France*. The first oboe player and the manager told us afterward that Mengelberg had told the men in no uncertain terms that they all owed a debt of gratitude to Monteux for bringing this colossal work for the first time to Holland, and that if he, Mengelberg, had studied it for weeks and months himself, he would never have been able to conduct it! It was after this event that he insisted Pierre share the season with him at the Concertgebouw.

Maestro will tell you in his own words of his years in this beloved old building in Amsterdam, where one meets the ghosts of Richard Strauss, Gustave Mahler, Hugo Wolf, Ottorino Respighi, Maurice Ravel, Claude Debussy, Vincent D'Indy, Georges Enesco, Bela Bartok, Willem Pijper, Arnold Schoenberg, Mauritz Rosenthal, Arthur Schnabel, Ignace Paderewski, Vladimir de Pachman, Emile Sauer, Harold Bauer, Alfred Cortot, Walter Geiseking, Teresa Careno, Jacques Thibaud, Eugene

Ysaye, Cesar Thomson, Bronislav Huberman, Sarasate, Fritz Kreisler, Arthur Nikisch, Hans Richter, Karl Muck, Bruno Walter, and so many others. The throng is overwhelming in its glorious immensity and artistry.

"In the month of September, in the year 1924, I received a telephone call from Mr. Samuel Bottenheim, the secretary and 'major domo' of Willem Mengelberg, whom I had met previously in New York and Paris, asking if it were possible for me to leave immediately for Amsterdam, as Mengelberg was ill. As it happened, my engagements in England, Sweden and Norway were later in that season, so I accepted to go to Holland with alacrity, as I was curious to know the great Concertgebouw orchestra and elated at the idea of conducting it. I was missing my Boston orchestra more and more, and this engagement offered me a sort of musical solace. I arrived in Amsterdam the last of September, and quickly established *rapport* with the Dutch ensemble. My first program was one I knew and loved, and I may say it was a fine success. It was on the ninth of October that I presented my first concert:

Overture to "Euryanthe" .... Carl Maria von Weber
Concerto for Violoncello .... Camille Saint-Saëns
Gerard Hekking, Soloist
Nuages et Fêtes, "Nocturnes" .... Claude Debussy
Symphony No. 4 .... Johannes Brahms

"Of course, the very fact that I was in Holland suggested to the music critics *Le Sacre du Printemps*, which had never been heard in the country. At that time the Concertgebouw Orchestra had an artistic manager and a business manager, both of whom became my dear friends. It was hard to deny any wish they presented. Dr.

Rudolf Mengelberg, the Artistic Director, and I worked together in complete harmony for years, and as for Dr. Paul Cronheim, the manager, we quickly established an *entente cordiale* that endures to this very day. (He later engaged me to conduct many operas for the Wagner Society of which he was the Secretary-General.) You can imagine my position when these two gentlemen begged me to conduct *Le Sacre* with their orchestra.

"I could not refuse. My, what work that was! This work which was a part of me seemed to have endless difficulties for the Dutch musicians. We persevered, and on the 12th of October played *Le Sacre* for the subscribers' Thursday night concert. We really played it, too; the heavy, rich strings of the orchestra suited the work admirably and I was truly thrilled by the sound. I have often regretted we have no recording of that eventful thirty-six minutes in the life of the orchestra.

"It was after these few concerts that Willem invited me to share the season with him. He was at that time conductor of the New York Philharmonic Orchestra, and consequently spent four and five months a year in America. During these months, I held forth in Amsterdam. He was a wonderful colleague. In the month of June every year, I would have a long conversation with him as to the programs for the following season. He invariably would say, '*Cher ami*, what will you play of Strauss?' Then with a shrug, he'd laugh and say, 'Oh, you choose the works you want to play and I will choose something else.' This was very easy for me, as you can well imagine. There was only one work I really had enough of during that decade. This was the Fantastic Symphony of Hector Berlioz, which Rudolf Mengelberg loved to the point of wanting it on the programs year after year." (*Caro*, this is true. Dr. Mengelberg would sit in my loge at the concerts, and during the slow movement of that formidable work close his eyes, and I often spied a tear coursing down his cheek.)

"I will never forget, and I smile every time I think of the visit I had in Paris from Jonkeer Anton Roell (at that time President of the Concertgebouw) and Dr. Paul Cronheim; their aim was to discuss my engagement as co-director with Mengelberg. I met these gentlemen at their Hotel Mirabeau and we had a delightful but business-like conversation as to my duties at the Concertgebouw, and my salary. We then enjoyed a magnificent meal together, proceeded on to the Moulin Rouge, which we all enjoyed immensely, thoughts of Toulouse-Lautrec in our minds and conversation. You may think, *chérie*, that we then went home to bed, but we decided that 'in Paris, do as the tourists do,' and went to the Rat Mort for champagne and a gay time. I, at last, gave up and went wearily home and to bed, while my two new friends finished their night at the Caveau Caucasian! The next morning at the appointed time of eleven o'clock I went again to the Mirabeau, to be met by a joyous and charming manager, Dr. Cronheim, full of stories of the early hours of that day. My new President appeared an hour later, excused himself for tardiness and explained he had but five hours sleep, which was quite enough in 'gay Paree.' I must say I wondered about a contract, used as I was to American ways, but no mention was ever made of such a paper, and I never received a contract or even a letter during the ten years I was at the Concertgebouw. A gentlemen's agreement sufficed."

Amsterdam, Holland,
November, 1963

Caro:

We are still here in Amsterdam, where the Maestro has been occupied the whole month with concerts and recordings with the Concertgebouw Orchestra. I need not tell you, who so completely understand the life we lead, that it is a joy to be here. My mind is obsessed day after day with memories of those years and full of reminiscences and musings of the sweet past, some joyous and some sad.

As the Maestro's engagement during those years was for four months only, we chose to live in Bruxelles, Belgium, because of its position between Paris and Amsterdam, strategic for us. It was also central for all Europe. This city is and was a small replica of the French capitol, gay and mondaine. We were especially intrigued by the combination of Flemish and Walloon culture encountered wherever we went in the small country. Our first home was in Bruxelles' loveliest suburb, Petite Espinette. From the Bourse (stock exchange) in the middle of the city, we took the Waterloo tramway and, if we could resist the allure of a glass of geuze (strong beer) and a fresh cottage cheese and onion sandwich at the fascinating café of the Moeder Lambeeck, we kept right on, past the Prince of Orange Hotel and the forest of Soignes, until we finally left the noisy, busy vehicle at our avenue. If the day was fine, however, we usually stayed on until Waterloo, the peaceful scene of Napoleon Bonaparte's great defeat by Wellington. It was thrilling to climb the great pyramid erected to commemorate the famous battle, and study the garish, painted panorama depicting the encounter of the two armies on the vast and fertile fields spread out before us.

Our home was a noble old house of faded brick, approached by a winding, tree-enclosed driveway. It was covered with clematis, wistaria and climbing ramblers. A wide lawn swept away to the gate, which was topped with a sonorous sounding bell. I loved this home, and always regretted leaving it, even for Holland, which of course I also loved. I must say, *caro*, our interior was very Dutch , à la Vermeer!

Many musicians from Bruxelles and Holland visited us at Petite Espinette, among them Désiré Defauw, the conductor; John Charles Thomas, then star of the Belgium National Opera the Monnaie; Willem Pijper, the Dutch composer; Francis de Bourguignon, the fine Belgian composer, and many others. One of our greatest joys in Bruxelles was to visit the palatial home of Eugène Ysaye, the renowned violinist. He was truly a colossal man, *caro*, monumental in every way. Feted throughout his life as one of the most astounding violinists the world has ever known, he carried his love of luxury and grandeur with him wherever he went, but it was especially noticeable in his own home on the Avenue de la Campagne. All the dinners were lavish, and a delight to the gourmet. The conversation was always of music, and many were the discussions (some of them heated, due in part to the copious quantities of wine and champagne served with the meals) over the right tempo for a quartet or concerto. Ysaye loved to play chamber music and since he then functioned as Maître de Chapelle at the Belgium court, we were often invited to small concerts at the palace on the rue Royale. Queen Elizabeth received vio-

lin lessons from Ysaye at that time, and played remark-
ably well. Princess Marie Jose played the piano in an
extremely professional manner also, and accompanied the
Maître very often. Because of the talent of these two royal
personages, the music at the palace was of superior quality, and it was a pleasure to attend concerts there.

I remember the first time I was invited with the Maestro to a chamber music concert in the royal home. I was
filled with excitement, and such trepidation! I practiced
speaking in the third person and held long conversations
with myself until I was sure I had mastered conversation
with royalty. That evening I decided no one would speak
to me anyway, and that I might as well relax and enjoy
the music and the beautiful room in which the concert
was given. Noticing a window seat partially enclosed by
a heavy silken curtain, I ensconced myself in it, beautifully concealed from the rest of the room. At last the
court entered; the guests stood until the King and Queen
were seated. I was delighted with my modest seat, from
which I could see and hear to perfection. The program
was principally delightful music of Monteverdi's time. I
closed my eyes and imagined myself at an ancient court
in Italy. I forgot my qualms over attending this concert,
when of a sudden I realized the music had stopped and
that people were conversing. King Albert and Queen
Elizabeth were walking slowly around the room, greeting the guests. A lackey passed me a glass of champagne
and a delicious small cake and I forgot to withdraw into
my little enclosure. At that moment the gracious Queen
approached with her lady-in-waiting, and I heard a
gentle voice say, "Madame Pierre Monteux, I believe."

I curtsied, and in a faint voice managed, *"Oui, votre
Majesté."* She smiled and asked, "You are an American?"

Again I answered, *"Oui, votre Majesté."* Thereupon her
Majesty proceeded to tell me of her voyage to the United
States during the war, asked me many questions, in the
answering of which I forgot about the third person, becoming more and more embarrassed at each *faux pas.*
Then very sweetly the soft voice said, "And if we simply
say 'you' to each other—?"

There are many stories of our life between the two
countries, *caro,* but when I asked the Maestro to "remember" a few incidents in Holland which either interested
or amused him, he said: "I think one of the artists I remember always with immense pleasure, even today, is
Moritz Rosenthal, the famous pianist. We spent many
delightful hours with him on the little tours with the orchestra in the Netherlands provinces, due to his wit and
bonhomie. Once, seated opposite him on our way to the
Hague, listening fascinated to his conversation on music
and art, I was startled almost out of composure to hear the
great pianist say, 'You know, Monteux, I think I will
really study and learn the Concerto in F Minor this
summer!' At that time Rosenthal was *seventy years old!*
I simply could not believe my own ears, and I said, 'Do
you really mean to do this?'

"He looked very serious, and answered, 'Yes, I want
to do it.' We both were silent for a while. I am sure he
knew I was conjecturing on the fact that he had made his
whole career and immense reputation as an interpreter
of Chopin and, as everyone knows, the Polish composer
wrote but *two* concerti for the pianoforte!

"Then there was Bronislav Huberman, the violinist so
popular in Holland at that time . . . I would always
receive a telegram just before the time allotted for his rehearsal for the concert with these words: 'You know it,

I know it, the orchestra knows it; will see you at the concert!' As this was very true, and as we had played it together very often, all went well at the concert, *Dieu merci!*

"Many were the artists who found it unnecessary to rehearse with us. Once we had engaged my old friend Jacques Thibaud, to open our season with the Beethoven Violin Concerto. He arrived the night before at a late hour and presented himself at the rehearsal the next day at twelve o'clock. We started to rehearse and both the orchestra and conductor were horrified at the performance of this most demanding of all concertos. I said, '*Mon ami*, what is the matter?' He answered, 'I haven't had time to work this summer, there have been so many golf tournaments.' I looked at him in amazement and replied with some heat, 'You'd better watch out, your golf will ruin your violin technique.' To my astonishment, he answered, 'I'm only afraid the violin will ruin my golf!' As you know, he made a great deal of money with his golf. He was nearly professional. Some good fairy seems to watch over artists, because he played that night, not as I would have had him play if he had been in fine form, but it was presentable.

"I have seen artists arrive for rehearsal with terrible colds, obliging them to use their handkerchiefs every two or three minutes, but the minute they started to play, the sniffling ceased, and the rehearsal and concert were completely free from any cold signs. They would then arrive in the *soloistenkamer* afterward and begin to sneeze, cough, and wipe at a great rate. Strange!

"I must tell you of my first meeting with Willem Pijper, the remarkable Dutch composer. As is usual with me, I was not satisfied with the supposedly 'new' music

being played in Holland at that time, and after conducting works of Cornelis Dopper, Alphons Diepenbrock and
Johannes Wagenar, composers popular and respected
throughout the Netherlands in the twenties, I began to
question certain critics and musicians as to the possibility
of finding a Dutch composer with a bit more originality
and daring in his compositions. I was told by many that
there was one named Pijper, but that he was '*sauvage et
un peu fou*' (crazy) and that he would not see anyone. I
decided this was just the fellow I must meet. I wrote him
three times, but received no answer. I then decided to
brave the tiger in his den, and one cold dark afternoon in
winter drove to his home unannounced.

"I must say I do not know what I should have done
without you, *chérie*, because you were really the one to
'screech' his mother down, and the reason for Pijper himself to come to the door. The old woman was not going
to let us enter. I will never forget his ascetic face, so thin
and white, with burning eyes that seemed to pierce one's
facade. There was no use in trying to placate Pijper with
cajolery. He seemed to see right through you, and in his
presence deceit was impossible. Do you remember how he
stared at us, and in an impatient voice asked us what we
wanted? I said, 'I want to know you and your music. That
is why I am here.'

"After what seemed minutes, he said, 'Oh you do, do
you? Well, come on in, then.'

"The entire conversation was in French which, to my
surprise, he spoke fluently. (I learned afterward that
most Dutch people speak good French.) He was very
bitter and spoke of the Concertgebouw *avec amertume*.
I am happy to say this attitude changed over the years,
and the artistic direction of that institution did every-

thing in their power to promote Pijper's music. He came often to visit us, both in Belgium and Les Baux en Provence, where we spent our summers, and later in Cormeilles en Parisis. He dedicated his Third Symphony to me, and I have always been very proud of this work. It has had success everywhere I have played it, especially so last year in Vienna at the Festival, where the Concertgebouw Orchestra gave a rousing performance of the work. The slow movement is hauntingly lovely, and to me it is Willem Pijper—tender and rather strangely resigned. I am extremely touched by it.

"I will never forget the occasion when Richard Strauss honored the Wagner Society and the Concertgebouw Orchestra by conducting an opera, *Tristan und Isolde* of Richard Wagner, and in concert a symphony of Mozart and his own *Till Eulenspiegel* and *Don Quixote*. I knew he was a great opera conductor, but I did not realize how truly magnificent he was until I heard three performances of *Tristan* under his direction at the Stadschouwburg in Amsterdam. Naturally I was thrilled at the idea of watching and hearing him conduct his own works, especially *Don Quixote*. I was a bit worried though, because we had a new violist from France who, though very good, had never played the exacting part for solo viola in this work. There were two or three other players new to the orchestra, also.

"At last the morning of the first rehearsal arrived. The whole orchestra was in place, ninety-seven musicians all ready for *Don Quixote*, which Dr. Rudolf Mengelberg and I supposed he would rehearse first, as it was the most difficult work on the program. But no! The Meister said in no uncertain terms, 'I shall rehearse Mozart this morning.' Which he proceeded to do, over and over. Every measure was rehearsed until the orchestra, who knew the symphony by heart, as they had played it many times with various conductors, were quite exasperated. After two hours of Mozart and a coffee break, as you call it, the great German meister played through at an unheard-of pace the poor *Don Quixote*, stopping but two or three times to explain that it must GO! The 'cellist was Marix Loevenson, the superb first 'cellist of the Concertgebouw Orchestra, who had played the work with Strauss and many times previous with Willem Mengelberg. He was, of course, very sure of himself. But I have never seen a viola player in such agony as was Frederic Denayer, the first viola. He was simply swimming through his Sancho Panza role. It was ghastly!

"Then the meister played *Till Eulenspiegel* from beginning to end without stopping once, saying, 'Oh, it's just one two, one two, all the time!'

"I must say that I was the one really to suffer from this lack of interest of Strauss in his own works, because I had to conduct the whole program the very next night in the Hague without benefit of a rehearsal. One cannot be more royalist than the king and, if Strauss was satisfied, there was nothing else for me to do: I didn't ask for a rehearsal, but I did take my two soloists for an hour or so that morning, just to acquaint ourselves with the work."

Caro, the Maestro could go on for days with his memories of the Concertgebouw and his ten years there, so we will continue in our next epistle and tell you why he left his beloved orchestra and of his years conducting for the Society Wagner.

London,
December, 1963

Caro Amico:

My thoughts go out to you in sunny Rome, these cold dark days when all England is covered with a heavy, dank blanket of fog. It even penetrated the Festival Hall this morning, where the Maestro was rehearsing for the Royal Philharmonic Society concert, to take place this week. The program is Brahms' Third Symphony, Berlioz Overture to *Benvenuto Cellini,* and my favorite of all Beethoven symphonies, the Pastoral. Maestro is to receive the coveted Royal Philharmonic Society Gold Medal. This is a tremendous honor, as this Society in its one hundred and fiftieth year of existence has seen fit to give but few Gold Medals.

I am very fond of the Royal Philharmonic Society, because once many years ago, when Beethoven was in dire need and very ill (indeed, I think it was his last illness), they sent him one hundred pounds, with the admirably thought up excuse that the great composer would project a tenth symphony! He had suggested a benefit concert.

Now this same Society is to make Maestro happy and proud as well as his whole London Symphony Orchestra. The medal is to be presented by Sir Adrian Boult, the famous English conductor, and I am elated because much of his presentation speech is taken from the book, *Everyone Is Someone,* which you know I wrote. Festivities here in England are always colorful and full of pomp and circumstance, and I look forward to this evening.

As I did not finish the Amsterdam years in my last

letter, we must return there, for I am sure you are interested in the operas Maestro conducted for the Société Wagner. They were many and varied. Dr. Paul Cronheim became the Secretary-General of this organization, whose only aim was to present operas in Holland with the finest artists possible, beautiful décors, and famed conductors who had *carte blanche* from the time of the opera's conception to the last performance. I do not remember ever hearing discussion of funds, and I know that some of the operas presented cost a pretty penny. I will never forget a certain *Carmen* given with new costumes, new scenery, and a complete French cast which Maestro gathered from all the opera houses of France, choosing each singer to fit vocally and physically the character he or she was to represent in the work. The role of Carmen was sung by Mme. Jeanne Bourguignon, a fine mezzo soprano and actress from the Pays Basque. She *was* Carmen. Dark hair and flashing black eyes, a Spanish beauty, exciting and satisfying in every way. Bruno Walter engaged her to sing the role soon after at Covent Garden.

This idea of the right personality for the role was carried into every work chosen by the Maestro. Mélisande was a simple young girl with a lovely voice, and I remember Maestro shaking her one day and repeating over and over, "You are beginning to feel a woman's emotions now—WAKE UP!" Pélléas was young and personable. Both singers made great careers afterward. The Mélisande was Janine Michaud, and the Pélléas was Martial Singher, a splendid artist.

Dr. Cronheim, who was a tremendous and untiring innovator, had the idea one year to present two operas, ancient and modern, in juxtaposition to each other. I

will let Maestro tell you of their decision and of the wonderful evening's entertainment they concocted.

"It *was* a wonderful evening, wasn't it? So full of charm
and gaiety. After much conversation and research, we
decided on *Acis et Galatea* of Jean Baptiste Lully, and
after the entr'acte, *L'Heure Espagnol*, of Maurice Ravel.
Dr. Cronheim insisted on authentic costumes and décor
for the Lully opera and we had interesting evenings por-
ing through tomes of old engravings having to do with
the operas of that time, both in Italy and France. He
revelled in all that was *fasteuse* and splendid, and I delight in theatre which has *panache*. You can imagine the
cordial relations which existed between us. Work under
conditions such as he created was a joy, and I went off
to France with enthusiasm to look for my cast.

"Ira Belline, Igor Stravinsky's niece, and Vera Sou-
deikine, now Madame Igor Stravinsky, a lady of impeccable taste and much imagination, created many of the
costumes for our operas. As they were both Russian, their
creations were vibrantly colorful, and as they had been
a part of the Paris scene for years they had real French
chic. A magical combination, *n'est-ce pas?*

"At that time we became acquainted with a brilliant
young French theatre designer, André Boll by name. Dr.
Cronheim and I journeyed to Paris one day to interview
him and to look at his maquettes for opera. We were
absolutely intrigued by his erudition in music, literature,
and art. Thus was started then and there a collaboration
lasting years. His *L'Heure Espagnole* was truly a joy, and
the public realized from the time the curtain was raised
on the scene of the old clockmaker's little shop that here
was a décor truly in harmony with the irrepressible, de-
risive music composed by Maurice Ravel. I really love to
conduct this little opera.

"Oh yes, that was an evening to remember, from every standpoint! I have had a few such evenings in my life in the theatre. *Fidelio* at the San Francisco Opera House was one, *Orpheus and Eurydice* in Amsterdam, with the wonderful English contralto, Kathleen Ferrier, as my Orpheus was another. I would also add *Falstaff* in Amsterdam with the most famous of all Falstaffs, the great Stabile, who told me one day that he did not know one note of music, and that he learned everything by repetition, over and over again until he knew it by heart! Of course, I had many good performances at the Metropolitan Opera House at different periods, but somehow there was always something either in the décors or in the singers chosen for the roles that displeased me. For example, a Mélisande beautifully plump, seen in her reclining position at the opening of the first act, looked for all the world like two small hillocks, round and shapely, on the floor of the stage. A far cry from the slender, adolescent damozel I demand for this role. Many times, also, music has played a secondary role. Alas!"

Caro, at this point the Maestro seemed lost in thoughts having to do with the vicissitudes of opera, no doubt. For my part, I shall never forget that night in Amsterdam when for a moment I dreamed I was in the theatre at the Palace of Versailles, assisting at a wondrous opera by the composer in vogue at that moment, Jean Baptiste Lully. Then of a sudden I was transported to Spain by the Estremadura, and Maurice Ravel with me. Of course we were in the loge at the State Theatre in Amsterdam and the Spanish Consul and all the elite of Holland were with us. Ravel was enchanted, as was the Dutch public.

The Spanish Consul, feeling that the Ravel opera called for a Spanish celebration, gave a beautiful supper honoring the composer and the artists, after the last presentation of the opera. Feeling the occasion called for a special evening dress, I asked my Paris couturier to design me a gown *très espagnole*. It was of heavy black satin with a long, tight bodice flaring forth into a wide flounce and train covered with inch wide black ruffles of the same material. It was a spectacular dress and I wore no jewlry, but tucked two red roses in my hair with a high black comb.

I felt gay and very Spanish as I entered the Consulate that night. The table was magnificent with large *épergnes* of red roses and white grapes, and white candles in antique silver holders. My chair at the right of the Consul was draped with an exquisite Spanish lace mantilla, as was the chair of the French star of *L'Heure Espagnole*. It was a joyful, elegant soirée, and my personal joy would have been complete had my feet not hurt, encased as they were in new black satin slippers. Immediately after the first course I slipped them off and, with a sigh of relief, settled down to an evening of gaiety. The food was delicious and the champagne cold and copious, the conversation was brilliant and the Consul gallant and charming. Well, all things, even the nicest, come to an end. When it was time to leave the festive board, I gingerly extended a foot to find my shoes, but alas! they weren't there! I stretched my leg farther and made a circular movement with my stockinged foot on the carpet. Then I made a pretense of reaching for my evening bag and peeked under the table. No slippers! I made frantic signs to the Maestro, who was making me signs that it was time to leave the table, of which I was only too well aware. I managed to smile, and as the Consul proceeded to the salon, I mentally thanked Vionnet for making my dress long. I followed the fascinating Spaniard, walking on tiptoe to look reasonably tall, and once in the salon, settled myself into a corner of a large divan with one foot under me and the other amply covered by my dress. I sipped my coffee and watched the butler, hoping he would make me a sign that my shoes had been found. He paid no attention to me at all, and occupied himself with the service of coffee and liqueurs. The Consul smiled and smiled throughout the rest of this now endless evening. I decided I would never ask for those slippers, and felt like Cinderella!

It was a snowy, cold winter night, and I thought of the wide Amsterdam sidewalks I would have to cross as I proceeded from door to motor and from motor to door. I left the Spanish Consulate in my stocking feet, walked valiantly through the fresh white snow to the car, then from the car into the hotel. When we got to our rooms, I rushed into the bathroom, pulled my satin skirts up around me, turned on the hot water tap and thrust my cold blue feet, stockings still on, into the delicious warmth. Needless to say, the Maestro thought I was absolutely mad. He says he will never forget *L'Heure Espagnole* for several reasons.

Early next morning, a huge box of red roses arrived, in the center of which were my satin shoes. A card therein read as follows: "*A Madame Pierre Monteux, femme charmante et* wonderful American sport! *Avec mes homages*, L.G. de C., *Consul de l'Espagne.*"

So many, many wonderful moments, *caro*, in our life in music. Holland was, and still is, the ideal country in which to make music. The orchestra is state subvented, and the conductor has nothing whatsoever to say about finances. When I consider the difference between this ideal state of affairs, and of the seventeen years we passed in beautiful San Francisco with the Symphony Orchestra there, where money, money, money was our *bête noir* and where every aspect of the orchestra's life was controlled by the budget, I realize that the ten years in Holland were halcyon indeed.

But one day in the year 1934, Maestro arrived home from a rehearsal in this paradise of music and announced in a weary voice, "I have had enough; I want to leave here and go on to new fields."

I gasped; it meant giving up a life I had grown to love: friends, the great orchestra, the lovely nostalgic country, and last, but not least, the finest and most remunerative position in all Europe. It meant more months of guest-conducting. I asked tremulously if anything had happened to motivate such a move. He said, "No, nothing has happened. I simply feel that if I am to grow, I must look for new fields to conquer. I must leave here, where everything is too easy and comfortable for me."

This was reasoning, *caro*, that I could understand; we had talked often of the necessity of artists moving on at times, and I could not help but feel he was right. I saw that he was worried as to my reception of this decision, and said quickly, in spite of a lump in my throat, "Of course we will go; I'm a bit tired and bored myself!"

The daily newspapers were sure that something had occurred between the management and Maestro, doing their best to make Dr. Rudolf Mengelberg the scapegoat. In spite of our denials day after day, we could not make them believe otherwise. Since Maestro was very popular, *Het Volk* and other papers tried to make a real issue of our departure.

Well, we left just before what was to have been the Maestro's tenth year jubilee. (I have a feeling, *caro*, that this jubilee might have had a bit to do with the momentous decision, as he simply loathes mile-posts.) We have been back many, many times, and never have there been other than the most cordial relations between the powers ruling the great orchestra, and Monteux. *Caro,* we go on to Paris in my next letter.

> Winterhaven,
> Hancock, Maine,
> Christmastide, 1963.

Caro Amico:

The rocky shores of Frenchman's Bay and all the inlets are edged with ice and snow. The evergreens are in their winter shroud of white snow, eerie ghosts in a world of deep green, gray and black; a still world with only the sound of myriads of birds; grosbeaks, juncos, starlings, sparrows, snowbirds, flashy blue jays, red-crested woodpeckers, gulls and many others crowding the feeders in the garden from morn till night. In the heavy quiet of the night I hear the great red snow plow, State property, ridding State road of the night's fall of frozen crystals, and I know that the highway will be clear, come morning, and all my small world will gleam and glint and glitter in the rays of the winter morning sunlight.

Christmas at home in Hancock is truly lovely, *caro.* There is the Holy Mass on Christmas Eve, when we all ride to Ellsworth, our county seat, through the wintry countryside to congregate with family and friends in the beautiful little church of St. Joseph on the High street. Candles, Christmas greens and poinsettias, white and red carnations in silver urns, joyous song from the choir, and above all the Mass, celebrating the Christ-

child's birth. Then the family tree, on Christmas morning with our three dogs and the cat participating. All
sparkle with the excitement of the moment. Hours of
crackling paper, shouts of pleasure and appreciation as
gift after gift is opened before admiring eyes. I think
the Maestro loves this moment even more than the children, so keen is his delight in each package unwrapped.

One needs a good rest after such merry commotion,
and we usually retire for a little nap in the peaceful atmosphere of Winterhaven, leaving children and grand-
children to carry on in the joyous clutter of tinsel, paper,
red and gold ribbons. At night, the fine dinner of traditional roast goose and ham, squash and potatoes from our
summer garden, peas with tiny onions and a flaming
plum pudding with hard sauce, made by our Mano! Two
fine wines, Chateauneuf du Pape and an old Mouton
Rothschild add to the delicious repast. After dinner Maestro insists on chilled glasses of Grande Marnier and we
sit, almost unable to move, I must admit, and talk quietly
of music. *Caro*, Christmas and Hancock really belong to
each other.

You are still in Rome, and though I am here in Maine,
I feel I must continue our Monteux story as you suggested in your last letter; in fact, it would be stupid to
leave the Maestro somewhere between Amsterdam and
Paris, I'm sure you will agree! This afternoon we motored over to Mount Desert Island, stopped at the pier
at Bar Harbor to eat our luncheon and while contem-
plating the islands in the bay, talked of the Orchestre
Symphonique de Paris, and of the years spent in fostering
music in the new Salle Pleyel.

"In 1929 I was asked by the Orchestre Symphonique de
Paris to conduct a season in the French capitol. This or-

chestra was founded in 1928 by a group of melomanes composed of bankers and socialites interested in an orchestra carefully chosen and amply subvented. The first concert was conducted by Louis Forestier; later the season was divided between Ernest Ansermet and Alfred Cortot. For some reason the concerts were not the success expected, and in the beginning of the year 1929 I received a letter from Alfred Cortot begging me to 'take over' the ensemble. I refused, stating that my engagement with the Concertgebouw Orchestra and many guest performances elsewhere would interfere.

"To my surprise, not a week later Cortot appeared in Holland and came to see me. He explained that the Banque Bénard and other very influential people were behind the orchestra; accordingly, I would have no financial worries at all, and I would have absolute *carte blanche* to do as I wished artistically. As you know, I gave in.

"I presented the first concert in 'April, 1929. If you remember, it was a colossal success. I little realized that it was also the beginning of years of terrible worries. *Quelle affaire!*"

The fact, *caro*, that the Maestro was to conduct four or five months a year in Paris hastened our decision to find a home in the country not too far from the great city. We searched for weeks, and at last found a wonderful old house in Cormeilles en Parisis, Seine et Oise. It was the ancient hunting-lodge of the famous Maréchal Ney of the Emperor's army. Its architecture of the First Empire was beautifully proportioned, gracious and dignified. There was a large rose garden, extremely formal, a fine orchard and vegetable garden in the rear. One entered through a great stone gateway into a courtyard green with ivy and moss-covered stones, an old stable and the servants' house to the left; to the right a small greenhouse and dovecote. We were enchanted with our purchase. We called it Vieux Murs.

The twenty-five foot pool in the center of the lawn lured all musical Paris, not to mention the swallows who bathed in the shallow tiny wash on its edge, night and morning, to the Maestro's delight. It was delightful to dine in our garden in the cool of the evening; there were many champagne parties on the lawn near the pool's placid water. The old walls of stone, covered with lichen and hoary with age, closed in our quiet, sylvan retreat. Sundays we had wonderful fêtes of quartet and ensemble playing, when the Maestro and friends played from early afternoon till late evening. Spaghetti cooked in chicken broth, with mushrooms and diced chicken in the sauce, large bowls of salad, a huge cheese tray and fruit tart always elicited salvos of praise and admiration for Fernande, our Belgian cook. This combination of music and food drew many friends from Paris and "points north," a joyful way to worship their twin gods, Bacchus and Apollo!

"The Orchestre Symphonique de Paris was in my estimation one of the finest orchestras I have ever conducted. Even today I think of it with a certain nostalgia. The major part of the ensemble were graduates from the National Conservatory, many no more than twenty-five years old. They possessed such brilliant virtuosity I often compared them to superb, intelligent race horses. The London Symphony Orchestra for the moment is comparable.

"During my second season with the orchestra, the two banks which were our main support failed. We were left with two or three generous Parisians as patrons, among them Mlle. Gabrielle Chanel, whom I shall always remember with affection and gratitude for her interest and largesse where we were concerned. Two of these patrons died at the year's end, and we were on our own. What to do? I could not let the orchestra die, especially while I was its director. We held a meeting and decided to go on in association, to run the concerts ourselves, and divide the profits at the end of each season. Usually the profits were so very small the director was forced to give his share to the general fund. Oh, I will never forget the vicissitudes of those years!

"I will tell you of two instances when I really thought I would give up. The great Russian composer-pianist, Sergei Rachmaninoff, had not played in Paris for a long time, and the committee of the orchestra thought it would be a magnificent attraction to present him in the Sunday concert at the Salle Pleyel. We counted on the White Russians living in Paris and the many Americans dwelling in the city and suburbs to fill our huge house. We were sure the advent of such an artist would be of outstanding success. The fee asked by Rachmaninoff's manager was exorbitant for Paris, but as we were practically sure of a full house, we decided to take a chance, and signed the contract. You can imagine our stupefaction on the day of the concert to see the Salle only half full. Despair is a better word. We knew we must pay the fee on the contract, and it was quite impossible due to the poor house. I decided to write Rachmaninoff a personal letter explaining our situation. I told him that the orchestra was in association, and that the profits divided at the year's end yielded a maximum of three thousand francs for each musician. (These were small, nearly valueless prewar francs.) I asked him as a gesture toward these French musicians to forfeit a part of his fee, calling his attention to the fact that after expenses were paid, there would be absolutely nothing left. The orchestra committee and I awaited his answer with impatience—and hope. At last it arrived and I opened it with haste, as I was extremely worried about the whole affair. The letter was very, very polite, full of compliments for myself and the orchestra, but—alas, the master "could not help us in our predicament; to do so would be contrary to his business rule, and after all there is a contract, *n'est-ce pas?*" As you know, the music director was forced to recognize the contract. *C'est la vie!*

"In regard to such happenings, we had a very disagreeable experience with another pianist, a very rich one, known for his splendid business acumen. Again the poor director and a friend came to the rescue of the orchestra! We simply could not let this magnificent ensemble disappear from the Paris scene. Indeed, it had become international. So international in fact that in 1932 we decided to take the orchestra to Berlin.

"No French orchestra had appeared in Germany since before the war of 1914. In our naive way, we thought our playing in Berlin would perhaps help soothe the fast deteriorating relations between the two countries. Mr. François Lang, the splendid young pianist who was later killed in World War II, was our soloist. Our first stop was in Brussels. The concert we gave in the Palais de Beaux Arts before King Albert and Queen Elizabeth made musical history. I have to smile when I think of the conversation I had with his Majesty during the intermission. He greeted me in his loge with a wide smile and said, 'Well, *mon cher Maître*, it takes a Frenchman to conduct our

national anthem, and we thank you; but the way you
played the *Marseillaise* this evening would give the innocent listener an idea that France was truly martial and
revolutionary, and of course, my dear Maître, this is not
true.' Then came a pause. 'Or is it?' He laughed loudly at
this bit of irony.

"I played the *Brabançonne* in a very dignified and
rather pompous manner, because I find it so. On the
other hand, our French national hymn when played by
this young orchestra—all, like myself, *poilu seconde
classe ordinaire*—received its just due; we abandoned
ourselves to a rousing *Marseillaise* fit to raise the roof of
the Palais de Beaux Arts. I was very proud when, that
evening, Les Dames Belges, famous feminine society created in World War I, presented me with a magnificent
copy of the Bruges Triptych. Their majesties stayed until
the very end of the concert, standing for minutes in their
loge, applauding our orchestra with enthusiasm.

"I often think of this evening when from my place on
the podium I have watched a part of the public rush to
the exits before I've had time to invite my men to stand
and receive the approbation of enthusiasts. The general
public does not realize the long hours of rehearsal every
concert entails. If they did, they would certainly show
greater appreciation to the artists on the stage. Applause,
long and loud, is sweet music to an artist's ears, and his
only way of knowing if the public liked his performance.

"On that tour, we gave concerts in Hamburg, Cologne
and Berlin. We had tremendous success in all three cities,
but Berlin was the climax. The cordiality and warmth of
the public was touching, and we were all elated. Never
have I heard the Fantastic Symphony of Hector Berlioz played as the Orchestre Symphonique de Paris

played it that night. (It has always been my opinion that the records of this work as played by that orchestra under my direction are by far the best I have ever made. I prefer to listen to those old recordings, even today.) In Berlin the public went wild after the *Scène aux Champs* (slow movement), an unprecedented mark of approval for the French woodwinds and tympani. When the symphony came to its dramatic end, the public rushed forward to the stage, crying, '*Vive l'amitié*, long live our friendship!' Hands were stretched toward us, many wept and waved handkerchiefs. This demonstration went on for seventeen minutes!

"We were profoundly impressed by this mass emotion for our music and felt that our tour had been more than a success. We could not believe there could be a war between our two countries ever again. Alas, just four months after this poignant episode, Adolph Hitler came into power and this same Berlin public with the same mass hysteria cried, '*Vive* Hitler, *vive* der Feuhrer!' and waved handkerchiefs and wept as they cheered. It was he who led *their* Fantastic Symphony to its bitter end.

"As we had no Board of Governors, and no Women's Committee looking for subscriptions and donations for us, we were obliged to look right and left for *des moutons à cinq pattes* (five-footed sheep). One bright day, we were offered that wonderful violinist, Nathan Milstein, who had never played in Paris and who wished to make his debut there with an orchestra before presenting himself in concert. He asked to play the Glazounov Concerto.

"Our announced program for that week included Schubert's Symphony in C major, adored by the French. I decided that if Milstein wished to play the Glazounov Concerto, I would change the program and make a fine one of Russian music only, thinking thereby to fill our coffers. I played the "Russian Easter" of Rimsky-Korsakof, and the Sixth Symphony of Tschaikowsky, the *Pathétique*, as the great work on the program. Well, the hall was full, and a large part of the public was drawn as usual from the Russian population of the city. Nathan Milstein played superbly, and his success was immediate and triumphal.

"Intermission, and then came the symphony. All was quiet until I started the delightful waltz in the third movement, when pandemonium broke loose in the hall. I turned and signalled for silence, and at that moment a deep and formidable voice bellowed forth from the second balcony in angry admonition: 'Monsieur Monteux, Maître, you should be ashamed to play that dirty music when you promised us the divine music of Franz Schubert!'

"I had no words to answer this devotee of Schubert. I played the last great movement of the Tschaikowsky symphony *con amore*, but the deep voiced man in the balcony had upset the Tschaikowskian thought. I still think that fellow had excellent taste, minus that word 'dirty.' However, all was not lost, and that week we received a superb article from a leading critic praising our unplayed Schubert. Ha, ha!

"I have grown to love the music of Tschaikowsky and feel I have a complete understanding of it, now. It has taken years. Too many interpreters of this Russian's music dwell on their personal *Sturm und Drang*, taking delight in the public's obvious sympathy and understanding of their own poignant suffering! Why wear one's self out parading in public one's own anguish, when it's all there in the music? I have learned to play Tschaikowsky's music as he wrote it and, I assure you, that is quite enough, quite enough. *Mais oui.*"

Caro, our life in Paris was quite unlike the intense, musical life of Amsterdam. There all our friends were in the entourage of the Concertgebouw. In Paris, almost all our friends were lawyers or politicians. Many of the French legislators are intellectuals. As Maestro is very much interested in world affairs, he enjoyed their brilliant conversation.

I think this recurring combination of art, literature and politics in French statesmen, rather rare in the world of political flim-flam, has in some ways profited the nation, but many times I have felt that good hard-headed political acumen would have been of greater use to France in the time of turmoil and chaos. Such men as Barthelémy, Deschanel, Claudel, Blum and Herriot were an honor to France, but I cannot help feeling their glory would have been greater if they had avoided the political arena and given the world the unadulterated gifts of their minds and spirits.

In no Frenchman was scholarly refinement and political aspiration so well combined as in Edouard Herriot. During the years we lived in Cormeilles and later in Paris, we grew to know and appreciate him as a noble personification of French culture and earthiness, at one and the same time. I must tell you about two memorable evenings with Herriot that exemplified both qualities.

We received a note one day from Mme. Yvonne Astruc, the French violinist, acquainting us with the fact that President Herriot (he was Président du Conseil des Ministres) wanted to read the manuscript of his *Life of Beethoven* to a few musicians—Monteux, Mme. Nadia Boulanger, Marcel Ciampi, the pianist and Mme. Astruc.

Thinking it would be a wonderful thing to have the President read his manuscript in her apartment on the Avenue Villiers, Mme. Astruc invited us all to dine there, suggesting to Herriot that we would all be delighted to have *souper* with him after the reading of the manuscript. He accepted, and we all arrived at Yvonne's beautiful home at half past seven. We sat down to dinner immediately, during which Herriot explained that his reason for wanting to read the book to musicians of wide sympathies and knowledge was to ascertain if "I have written any imbecilities or musical errors in this life of the greatest of all composers."

After dinner we settled ourselves in comfortable armchairs, a small pot of coffee on a tabouret near each listener. The President sat in a huge, high-backed chair, and light from a floor lamp diffused a soft glow on the manuscript spread on a table in front of him. His fine voice, deep and resonant, filled the room, and we listened fascinated as the life of the master composer became reality through the words written by Edouard Herriot, French statesman. At intervals the President would stop to fill his pipe and the listeners would drink some strong coffee and change their positions.

Page after page of the precious manuscript fell on the table. The vibrant voice was full of emotion and the hand holding the remaining leaves trembled as he described in magnificent language the death of the master. When at last the dying Beethoven breathed his last, a deep sigh filled the room on the Avenue de Villiers and no one spoke for several minutes. It was the President himself who broke the semi-trance by saying, "*Eh bien, mes enfants,* it is four o'clock. Thank you for your patience. Shall we eat?"

Later at the restaurant the President questioned us, demanding to know what mistakes he had made. Nadia and Monteux looked at each other and said in unison, "There was not one, not even a small one, Monsieur le Président!"

The other occasion was a gala concert we gave in Paris with the Orchestre Symphonique de Paris. We were the first in France or anywhere else, I think, to present dancers with a symphony orchestra. We gave one gala with the famous and popular Spanish dancer, Argentina, and the Maestro played wonderful music of Granados, deFalla, Turina and Albeniz—a tremendous success. Because of this, we decided to present "Homage à Diaghilev" with Serge Lifar, premier dancer of the Paris Opera, as soloist.

The program consisted of Igor Stravinsky's *Petrouchka*, and Ravel's *Daphnis and Chloe* in its entirety. Serge Lifar danced the solos of the *Fils Prodigue* of Serge Prokofiev. We found in one of the theatre warehouses in Paris a huge curtain made of a sort of tulle. It was off white in color and served our purpose admirably. Maestro sat the whole orchestra far back on the stage, leaving ample room for the dancer. When the orchestra played the two ballets of Stravinsky and Ravel, the curtain was wide open. When closed for the dancer, one could see the instruments through its diaphanous folds, with bits of brass and silver showing here and there. The effect was strange and splendid. This was an extremely brilliant program, and the moment the posters appeared on the boulevards we were besieged for tickets and were sold out in four days!

One morning our telephone rang. I was surprised to hear the voice of the President's secretary. She said his

Excellency had read the program of the "Homage" and would like very much to attend the concert. Would it be possible for me to invite him to my loge? I replied that I would be delighted and honored. I awaited the gala with impatience. Not only was I to hear fascinating and brilliant music and watch a superb dancer, but I was to have the company of the most brilliant and talked of man in Europe.

That evening the Salle Pleyel was literally packed with the most elegant audience Paris had seen in months. Nearly everyone was in full dress. I thought, "This is really a night worthy of Diaghilev, how very wonderful!" I noticed, as I entered my loge, Princess de Polignac, the Comtesse de Noailles, Missia Sert and many others. The concert was due to start at nine o'clock and precisely five minutes before the hour, the President arrived. He wore a wrinkled gray business suit and carried a large package wrapped in newspapers. He whispered, "*Bon soir, mes homages, Madame,*" then slipped into the place I had reserved for him in a corner of the loge, taking precaution to place the parcel well under the chair. Of course, everyone in the hall recognized Edouard Herriot. I nearly burst with pride, as the ladies stared at the great man through their raised lorgnettes.

The atmosphere in the hall was close, and as the concert progressed it seemed stifling to me. To add to my misery, I seemed to smell an odor of fish. Then a strange, heady smell of something else emanated from the bundle under the President's chair. It was so awful that the ladies in the loge to my left eyed us with disgust. The very chic Parisiennes in the loge to our right glared at us in revulsion.

I was mortified, but the President was in heaven, his

eyes closed during the *Daphnis and Chloe* music, a smile of complete satisfaction on his face.

At last the verbal innuendoes of the ladies and gentlemen surrounding us were impossible to ignore. I whispered to my famous guest, "Monsieur le Président, what have you in that package which smells so very peculiar?"

He laughed and said, "There is cheese, and a few lobsters a friend brought me from Dieppe, and as I passed the store of the Café de Brasil I also bought a few pounds of fresh coffee to take home to Lyon!" He was then, as he had been for years, Mayor of Lyon. It was his intention to take the midnight train for home after the concert. He was not aware that there was anything unusual in carrying cheese, lobsters and coffee to a gala soirée; for him, only the music was important.

During the long years of the war, when Edouard Herriot was imprisoned by the Nazis, I thought often of the package under the chair in the Salle Pleyel, and received comfort from the knowledge that the great Frenchman, secure in his intellectual superiority, was truly safe in his own tower of the spirit.

Caro, in my next I will tell you of the first school of conductors in Paris.

V

SCHOOL FOR CONDUCTORS—
SAN FRANCISCO SYMPHONY
—MONTEUX IN ISRAEL

Winterhaven,
Hancock, Maine,
January, 1964

Caro:

The wind howled dolefully all day yesterday. In the afternoon we sat by the fireplace, cups of hot tea and plates of molasses cookies to cheer us, and talked of Paris and the first School for Conductors. Maestro spoke at length about this, his most cherished project. I am sure you will be interested, *caro*, as you know what the school means to him. Do you remember, he told you that it is "the most important thing" in his life as a musician?

I had long dreamed of a school for conductors in conjunction with the Orchestre Symphonique de Paris, and one day I broached the subject to Mme. Yvonne Astruc, who had a fine school for violinists, with the great composer-violinist, Georges Enesco, as the master-teacher. Maestro and Georges Enesco had been friends for years, and as I knew they admired each other's musicianship, it seemed to me ideal that they teach in the same school. Mme. Astruc was delighted with the plan, as was Enesco, and we accordingly sent a few notices to different European papers. The first week we received twenty-seven letters demanding full particulars. I answered immediately, and in spite of Maestro's incredulity, opened the June session with twenty-three bona fide pupils in the art of the baton. This was the beginning of Maestro's teach-

[173

ing young men his beloved art—from the Ecole Monteux in Paris in 1932, to the present Domaine School for Conductors in Hancock, Maine. Thirty-two years in all. He will tell you in his own words of the school:

"For many years I had been troubled by the lack of discipline in many of the young conductors I had watched in concert. They were completely ignorant of the true and noble *métier du chef d'orchestre*. Indeed I felt that most used their position to exteriorize pent-up emotions and make a show of themselves! Exponents of Jacques Dalcroze and eurythmics, perhaps, but not trained and able conductors, knowing music from A to Z, having knowledge of the intricate technique of the baton, able in every way to help their orchestra execute their demands as having to do with the requirements of the music, and above all, instilling in their orchestra the dignity of their profession.

"The conductor's baton is his bow; it continues the right arm. It is, when well used, extremely precise, certainly more so than five fingers waving in the air! Because of it, men sitting at the back of the orchestra feel at ease, especially when they have many measures to count in their music. (I have been told this by many orchestra musicians over the years.) The baton is at times electric and exciting, at other times dainty and elegant. To use the entire arm continually throughout a concert must be extremely tiring, and is apt to confuse the orchestra and tire the beholder. I remember discussing this question with my old friend, Arturo Toscanini, when crossing the ocean together. 'But caro Monteux, it is with our beautiful baton we make the music; we play on our great instrument the orchestra with it; the more expert we are with it, the finer the music.' I absolutely agree.

And so, it is a law that all who come to the Domaine School for Conductors must bring a baton, and I do my best to teach them its use. It has been written that one recognizes a Monteux pupil by his use of this delicate wand. I hope so.

"In Paris we used a part of the orchestra twice a week for our lessons. At the end of every season, the orchestra chose the winner to receive their prize. This prize consisted of a diploma, and, best of all, a public concert with the whole orchestra in the Salle Pleyel. For three years, no one was chosen. I insisted they be extremely critical, and believe me, they were. After three years, they finally chose Charles Bruch, now the conductor of the French National Radio Orchestra in Strasbourg. As second prize, James Sample, at this writing the fine conductor of the Erie, Pennsylvania Orchestra. Bruch conducted a superb concert in the regular concert series and has continued his career, guest-conducting all over Europe with great success. I have enjoyed conducting his well trained Strasbourg orchestra many times.

"A few years ago, Olin Downes, music critic of the New York *Times*, asked me to be judge, with a few other gentlemen, of a contest to choose a young conductor. He asked who I thought would be good judges. I said, two concertmasters, two members of the woodwind section of an orchestra, two members of the brass section, two tympanists and two stringed bass players. I said, 'You do not need me. They will judge your young aspirants very well, I assure you. Frankly, they are the only ones to judge competently.' He was very surprised.

"Yes, I worked very hard with the Orchestre Symphonique de Paris, and for a while it was one of the outstanding orchestras of Europe. To receive help from the government, other than six thousand miserable francs, I had to play three hours every year of first auditions of French compositions! I solved this problem by announcing a concert of premières. These were really wild, as all those young and eager for sensationalism filled the hall to overflowing. At one of these concerts, I played the overture to *Les Eumenides*, a stark, archaic work by Darius Milhaud. I had not played the last note when the public started to roar approval from the balconies, disapproval from the floor. Cries of 'bis bis,' from the balconies, 'Shut your traps' from the floor. It was scandalous.

"After a few minutes I gave the entrance signal to Maurice Maréchal, the magnificent 'cellist who was to play the 'Cello Concerto of Arthur Honneger in first audition. He was greeted by shouts and boos from the ardent Milhaud fans in the balcony, who were insistent on hearing *Les Eumenides* again. I held up both hands to quiet them, and at last, when there was silence, I said, 'I understand many would like to hear *Les Eumenides* again.' '*Oui, Non, Oui, Non, Non.*'

"I again asked for silence, and continued, 'Please permit me to go on with the concert, and I will play the Milhaud ouverture for all who wish to hear it *at the end of the concert*. Those wishing to hear it may remain, and those to whom it seemingly gives no pleasure may leave.' Every one stayed—not a soul left. Ha, ha!

"I must say my public everywhere has been demonstrative. I would often say, after a concert that had been received with polite applause, 'What a boring public that was, do you think the concert was boring, also?' Oh, yes! The public in Paris were always with me, but alas! the various governments paid little attention to me, or to the

Orchestre Symphonique de Paris. I was told that my name in their lists of artists had the words '*pour l'exportation*' written after it. It is true I was sent north, south, east and west. I even spent two months of one winter in Soviet Russia, where I startled the natives by playing works of Stravinsky and Prokofieff they had never heard. But that is another story.

"In the winter of 1928 I went to the Philadelphia Orchestra and was there until April. Here also I succeeded in offending a large part of the conservative public by a magnificent account of *Le Sacre du Printemps*. It is inconceivable today, yet literally half the audience vacated the old Academy of Music during and after the poor Rites, which they obviously detested. I remarked to a journalist that it was my opinion that 'but five percent of the afternoon public came for the music.' This caused a tremendous stir, and I was even told by my manager that I should never have said such a thing. I replied that I was sure *all* the ladies considered themselves in the select five percent! That was 1928 and now it is a different story; the public is so very music-minded the conductor has the feeling at times of playing to an audience of critics!"

Caro, I must tell you of our departure from Russia. The Leningrad Orchestra all came to the station to see us off, many bearing gifts. It was all very gay and sad, sad and gay. I was too worried to be either.

A young man having to do with the orchestra, now unhappily dead, asked me to take a letter to his brother, who had been the Czarist ambassador to the court of Norway. He had not seen this older brother for years, and was desirous of sending him the family's news. I, on the impulse of the moment, said I would be delighted to take a letter to the ambassador. Absolutely sure I was on a secret mission, I did not breathe a word of our conspiracy to Maestro and hid the little envelope on my person, beautifully sewn into the hem of my underskirt. To say I was nervous at the station and again at the frontier, *caro*, would be a real understatement. I truly didn't have a minute's peace until I found myself over the frontier and in Finland.

Here a very tall, stern Finnish customs man asked me in Finnish if I was carrying anything on me. This I understood, as he pointed to his clothes, then to mine. I asked, *"Parlez-vous français?"* He shook his head, and in a gruff voiced growled, *"Nein, Deutsch."* At that time I did not speak German, and asked the Maestro what I should do. He said, "Well, sing him some of the Schumann lieder."

I stared at him in amazement but happily got the idea, and in a saccharine voice told him of Maestro's *"Ring an meinem Finger,"* bought *"im wunderschoenen Monat Mai,"* and so on until the austere Finn burst out laughing and motioned for us to board the train. I'm sure he often told the story of the crazy French lady who sang German songs at his frontier.

At last we arrived in Helsingfors, tired, cold and hungry. It was five o'clock in the morning. We sat in the station dining-room drinking delicious hot coffee. It was here I divulged my duplicity to Maestro. Needless to say, *caro*, he was horrified! In the middle of his scolding, a man approached our table and asked us in good French if we were artists. I said that Maestro had been conducting in Russia for two months. He said he knew it, and called Maestro by name. He introduced himself as the Station-Master and asked us if we would like to meet Sibelius,

the great Finnish composer. We said we would be delighted and honored. You can imagine our surprise, *caro*,
when he said, "I will telephone his home at seven
o'clock." We thought this an imposition, but he said,
"Absolutely not. I know he will be very happy to see
you." Well, he telephoned, and it appeared Sibelius was
away in the country. Then the Station-Master telephoned
Robert Kajanus, the conductor of the Helsingfors Orchestra, and we had an enjoyable visit with him at his
fine home.

After two concerts in Stockholm, we proceeded on to
Oslo, Norway, where the Maestro was to conduct a few
concerts and I was to deliver the famous letter. I was
worried throughout the voyage, as the Russian government had not paid us on leaving the U.S.S.R. and our fees
for the two months of concerts made a considerable sum
of money in American dollars. Oh, I was sure *they*
had no intention of ever paying us for all those concerts. Maestro was not so sceptical, and reminded me that
even if we weren't paid I had *seen* Russia, the splendid
Hermitage Museum, the palaces of Nicholas II and many
other marvels in the cities of Leningrad and Moscow. He
did not seem the least bit worried.

We were told in Russia that we would be paid by a
bank in Oslo, but after five days in Oslo there was no
word from a bank of any kind. I decided to contact the
French government, but on the morning of the sixth day
a notice came from the bank, and we presented ourselves
with our credentials. We were ushered into the president's room, drank aquavit and conversed for what
seemed to me an interminable time. There was no talk of
money however! As the president at last arose to bid us 'Au
revoir,' we started out the door, the Maestro puzzled and

I furious. Then he cried, "Oh, I forgot a little something —ha ha!" and handed us a huge envelope containing thousands of good American dollars. I sighed with relief; then Maestro made a typical remrk: "It's going to be boring to have to take care of all that money until we get to Paris!" Money has always bored him.

The next day I telephoned the former Russian ambassador, who had turned his embassy into a *pension*. I told him I had a communication for him from his youngest brother, and we accordingly made an appointment for the next afternoon. When we arrived at the *pension*, we were received by a huge, extremely imposing man who greeted us with true old world courtesy. A little maid in a worn uniform brought us tea. After the banalities were over, the ambassador leaned toward me and asked, "Well, and how did you find it in Russia?"

I told him of our enthusiasm for all the beautiful and magnificent things we had seen, which seemed to please him. Then I said, "It is wonderful, Excellency, the effort being made to educate the people. All the museums are full of pupils with their teachers."

I had hardly spoken the word "teachers" when his great fist pounded the table, his face became purple with rage, and he literally yelled at me in a terrible voice which shook the room, "*Éduquer le peuple, éduquer les bêtes!* (Educate the people, educate beasts!)"

I said *sotto voce* to Maestro, "Now I understand much better than I did. Let's go." And we did, bowing deeply to the representative of Nicholas II as we passed by him on our way to the street.

It was in Oslo I stopped smoking, *caro*. It is not difficult. All one needs is to be told one smells like a man, and that "Chanel No. 5 would smell much better" by one's nearest and dearest. One goes to the bathroom, thinks it over, lifts up the window and drops into the snow below one's jade lighter, one's jade cigarette holder, one's leather holder with its package of cigarettes and with them one's yearning for tobacco. This sacrificial act I have never regretted, as I came to agree that Chanel No. 5 and other perfumes are without a doubt more feminine smells to a man who has never smoked, and who loathes cigarettes!

And so I gave up a vice, and we then returned to Paris by way of Amsterdam. I had been commissioned by De Telegraf to write the story of our Russian visit and you can imagine my pride in seeing it published. I am not sure my articles pleased our Russian hosts, for memories of rags, beggars, bad food and bed bugs recurred again and again in my story. There were many episodes during the years from 1928 to 1934 I would have pleasure in telling you, *caro*, but this has been a long letter and I want you to receive it before you leave Rome. I shall tell you in my next of our return to the United States.

Hancock
Maine
January, 1964

Caro:

   ˈ We are preparing to leave our home in Maine for another stay in Europe. Today I look out the window at a white world. The evergreens are heavily laden with snow, their beautiful branches touching the ground. This light feathery snow pleases our James, as the electric plow tosses it to the sides of the paths and driveway, two sprays of white crystals which fall in pristine purity on the lawn as he passes. What heavenly peace is to be found in a country snowstorm, Caro.

The evenings are long, though the day has one hour more of light since we came here in December. I have profited from the evening hours and, as Maestro sipped his Grand Marnier, we have talked of the return to America and of the three months spent in Los Angeles, before going on to San Francisco.

"In the fall of 1934, I was invited by Otto Klemperer, conductor of the Los Angeles orchestra at that time, to conduct five weeks of concerts in southern California, while he conducted a series of concerts with the New York Philharmonic Orchestra. I was very happy to renew contact with American orchestras, though I must say, I have never been too fond of southern California. I left my heart years ago in the northern forests on the slopes of the Sierras, where the great redwoods touch the sky and where one can dream away hours in the Cathedral-like silence. However, it was good to know that I was wanted in America and I looked forward with real excitement to meeting the musicians of the Los Angeles Philharmonic Orchestra, of which I had heard fine reports. I was not disappointed. The orchestra was very fine indeed. I have had the pleasure of working with them many times since and have found them extremely co-operative, acquiescent and enthusiastic—an excellent ensemble.

"During my engagement, I received a letter from Leonora Wood Armsby of Burlingame, California, requesting an interview with me at my earliest convenience, as she had 'something very important' to ask of me. I knew Mrs. Armsby, as she had once engaged me to conduct a series of summer concerts in San Mateo. I answered that I would be delighted to talk on any subject.

"Mrs. Armsby was a charming lady, lovely to look at and interesting to converse with, especially when the subject was music, which was her abiding passion. I was sure she would ask me to become the conductor of the San Francisco Symphony Orchestra, as I had heard many rumors to that effect. I knew the orchestra was in a lamentable condition and that it was only playing for the radio hour concerts given every Sunday evening under the sponsorship of the Standard Oil Company of California. (This company did much through these concerts to save the fine nucleus of the ensemble, which in the past had so nobly functioned under the leadership of Alfred Hertz, who had been a magnificent Wagnerian conductor at the Metropolitan Opera.) Therefore, I was not surprised when Mrs. Armsby appeared at the old Hollywood Hotel, former home of many famous cinema stars of the nineteen twenties, accompanied by Mr. Peter Conley, manager of the orchestra.

"Without mincing words (she was the daughter of a judge and definitely not given to verbosity), she told me that my old friend, Mischa Elman the violinist, had urged her to prevail upon me to take over the San Francisco Symphony. Elman knew of my struggles in Boston and Paris and insisted I was the one to give the orchestra new impetus and prestige to the music life of the beautiful city he so loved. His charming wife Helen was a San Franciscan and they spent many happy days there. Mrs. Armsby, who had lived in New York during my Boston years, begged me to 'give it a try,' saying she knew I would succeed.

"After Mr. Conley had explained the situation from

his point of view, that is to say, the business side of the question, they told me in glowing terms of the magnificent Opera House, built as a War Memorial, the palatial home of the Orchestra; of the outstanding soloists in the Orchestra; of the fascinating city that San Francisco was; of the joy of living there; of the thousands of music-lovers 'dying' for real Symphony concerts again; and of various other aspects of northern California aimed to intrigue me.

"At last they ceased speaking, looking fixedly at each other and, in the embarrassing silence which ensued, Leonora Armsby leaned toward me and in a very small appealing voice said, 'Mr. Monteux, I must tell you that we have only twelve thousand dollars with which to start our season in January. We feel if we can announce your engagement, the situation will look much different in no time!' I told them I should have to consider their offer, which you must admit was not a very brilliant one! It would mean that I give up the Orchestre Symphonique de Paris, my school, our home there, work very hard to rebuild a solid organization again, isolate myself from possible engagements in Europe and elsewhere, and accept a whole new burden which looked visionary, to say the least. They departed with the promise they would hear from me within a week's time.

"Well, as you know, I can never resist a challenge. I accepted, though I must say to you, *chérie*, without great enthusiasm for this engagement!" (This was very true. I had the feeling that once out west, with the vast waters of the Pacific Ocean staring me in the face, I would be completely estranged from my world, which was the east coast of the United States and the old Europe which I loved so deeply. I felt no affinity for the west at that time. I knew I would miss the Atlantic: I considered it

"my ocean," and the countries on both sides of its wide-
spread blue green water were my heritage from ancestors
who "followed the sea" in years past.)

"I arrived in San Francisco the first week of January,
1936. That week I listened to the orchestra in a broad-
cast conducted by my dear friend Gaetano Merola, director of the San Francisco Opera Company. I think
San Francisco and indeed the whole of California owe
more to Merola than any other artist. He had vision and
enthusiasm, a winning personality and the true Italian's
love for fine opera. Above all he loved San Francisco and,
because he was tireless, literally gave his life to the city
which reminded him incessantly of Naples.

"After his concert we discussed the musicians then in
the orchestra. I decided then and there to give Naoum
Blinder, the concertmaster, a long contract. He was
superb; I think him without a doubt one of the finest leaders I have ever encountered." (He is also an astounding
teacher of the violin. Isaac Stern and many other fine
soloists on this lovely instrument have attested to Blinder's
superior pedagogy.)

"As with Boston, it was necessary to make many addi-
tions as the orchestra had been severely diminished by
the exodus of many musicians to the studios in Hollywood
where work was steady and the pay excellent. Unhappily,
I found there were very few truly first-class musicians
of symphony calibre to choose from in the Bay region.
The Musicians Union at that time was very strict in regard to imports. I must say, they were never very helpful. In the seventeen years I was at the head of the orchestra, I was allowed by the Union to import less than
a half dozen musicians from the east. Bruno Walter once
made the remark that he could not fathom how I had

made an orchestra, which received nothing but praise
from all the critics of the United States and Canada on
their tour of these two countries in 1947, with the elements I had recruited from northern California! At that
time the greater part of the San Francisco Union members consisted of jazz drummers, banjo, guitar, ukulele
and saxophone players!

"Well, before I could be granted an importation of a
musician from the east or elsewhere, all local musicians
applying for the vacant place had to be heard. These auditions took place before an incredible committee of Union
members! It was seemingly not enough that *I* found the
musician inadequate! To support this attitude on the part
of my 'brothers' in the San Francisco Union, demanded
a patience I found hard to muster at times. The mediocre
musician must be protected, according to the Union. We
cannot all be geniuses, I know, but a difference should
be made between the artist who has worked for years to
perfect his art and the lesser man who obviously has
neither the talent nor the necessary stamina to work. I hear
that this rule against importations has changed in San
Francisco and that my successors have profited by the
change. I only wish my 'brothers' had made this change
during my tenure with the orchestra. We could have
reached great heights together.

"When I arrived in San Francisco, the minimum
wage of the orchestra players was sixty-five dollars a
week. When I left, it had been raised progressively to
one hundred and five dollars. I hear it is much more at
the present time. Of course this fee included all the players, even the musician playing the three notes on the
triangle!

"I gave my first concert with the San Francisco Symphony Orchestra on the tenth of January, 1936. The program consisted of the Bach-Respighi Passacaglia in C minor; three Nocturnes of Claude Debussy, *Nuages, Fêtes,* and *Sirènes.* (For the Debussy I used the Municipal Chorus. The chorus of women's voices had been beautifully rehearsed by the fine conductor, Mr. Hans Leschke with whom I worked in complete and affectionate harmony for many years.) After the intermission we played Beethoven's Seventh Symphony. The following day, the local papers told of the success of our first concert in their headlines: 'New Conductor Works Miracles with Orchestra as Season Starts . . . Ovation Won by Monteux. . . . Orchestra at its Best . . . There Is a Symphony Orchestra Again in San Francisco!'

"We had worked very hard, indeed. Throughout the long years, the Orchestra always gave me of their best. There grew between us a deep affection which carried us through many trials and tribulations. I remember them all with true fellow-feeling.

"Olga Samaroff, the noted pianist, made the remark in a speech at a dinner given for me in New York, that 'It's not where you are that counts, it is what you accomplish where you are, and Monteux has proved this to be true in San Francisco.' Our RCA Victor records were at the top of the sales list and we were considered, rightfully, one of the big five among American orchestras.

"During the war years we had full to over-flowing houses, due to the influx of service men and officers. These years were very exciting. Both Mrs. Armsby and I knew that at the war's end there would come a letdown, and that something had to be done to circumvent this eventuality. I suggested to her one day that I had been there ten years, and that perhaps it would give new impetus if another conductor were engaged. (My New York manager had been insisting that I was 'lost' on the west coast, and frankly I was looking forward to a return to concerts in Europe.) She was adamant that I stay on until 'things got back to normal.' I told her that I had restored the orchestra to its former place among the American ensembles, I had given the public the best of the classics, and a suitable allotment of modern compositions as far as the budget permitted. I had but one desire left—to show what I had accomplished to the rest of the United States and Canada. For this chance, I would stay on a while longer. After many meetings, an immense amount of talk and planning, I was accorded permission to make the grand tour of the country, including all the large and important cities en route.

"I conducted fifty-three concerts in fifty-six days! My pupil, James Sample, at present conductor of the Erie, Pennsylvania orchestra, assisted at times by conducting various works in cities here and there, to relieve me. This tour brought us renown beyond our expectation and I was very proud when the State Legislature voted me Ambassador-at-Large for the State of California. All this was very gratifying. Shortly after this I received two doctor's degrees, from the University of California and Mills College. All these honors were topped off by the coveted Fellowship from Stanford University.

"At last, in 1950, when I had been in San Francisco fifteen years, I told Leonora Armsby I had been offered many concerts in Europe and the east, and that I felt it was really time for me to go. She answered that she intended to leave in a year or so, and begged me to stay, saying, 'We will leave together.' I acquiesced, and consequently left the orchestra in 1952. (I returned to San

Francisco shortly after, with the Boston Symphony Orchestra, on their first American tour after the war.) I
feel I should have relinquished my post at the end of the
war, but there was no refusing Leonora Wood Armsby
who was the soul of our organization.

"I had only been in San Francisco a few years when
Mr. Peter Conley died. Mr. Howard K. Skinner was engaged to replace him as manager, and I have vibrant
memories of our years of ardent work together for the
orchestra and music education. It was he who organized
our tour and bore the heavy burden of the financial worries during our trek across the country. Our *bête noir* was
the eternal budget—money, money, money! It seemed
we never had sufficient to meet our needs which, believe
me, in comparison with other orchestras in the country,
were modest. A few families gave generously to the orchestra, but the major part of the individual gifts were
less than one hundred dollars each year. The large gifts
were mainly given by the old aristocratic Jewish families
of the city, all music lovers and extremely cultured.
Many of these distinguished persons were on the Board
of Governors of the Orchestra. I do not know how we
would have existed without their enthusiastic support and
encouragement. Another group from the 'Peninsula'
gave us fervent and altruistic comprehension and aid.
This group, headed by Mr. and Mrs. George Cameron,
owners of the San Francisco *Chronicle*, Mr. and Mrs.
Charles Blythe, Mrs. Benjamin Lehman and others were
extremely consistent in their support of our work. I am
indebted to all who helped us so willingly throughout the
years.

"It seemed though that we were always begging for
the orchestra. I feel this manner of supporting and aiding

symphony orchestras and art museums absolutely wrong
and harmful. I strongly believe we must have a Ministry
of Fine Arts or its equivalent in the United States. These
institutions, so necessary to the cultural life of the country, should as in Europe be supported by the government,
thus alleviating the burden which falls on a select few.
There is something incongruous in begging for beauty.
I assure you it is very embarrassing for a fine, talented
musician, an artist worthy to play in a first-class orchestra, to meet each year in his perigrinations through his
home city such posters as I saw in San Francisco throughout the years—appeals that shamed both reader and musician: Keep Your Symphony from Dying . . . Come to
the Aid of Your Orchestra . . . Without your Urgent
Aid, No Symphony . . . and so on. To me, this way of
doing is extremely distasteful.

"Many of our concerts were given in the hideous and
huge Civic Auditorium, a monstrosity both to contemplate and play in. It contained ten thousand seats! These
concerts were 'bought' by the city, which taxes the population one half of one per cent, supposedly to support the
San Francisco Symphony Orchestra. However, in spite
of the fine concerts given by the orchestra and paid for
by this money, it was a drop in the bucket when compared with the over-all expense of running the organization. This money I believe is now used for the summer
Pop Concerts conducted with great success by Arthur
Fiedler. There have been misunderstandings about this
tax fund. I think it caused us a loss of many gifts at one
time, as people thought it must surely be enough to keep
the orchestra out of the red, arguing: 'Why give more,
when we are already taxed?' Money was our *bête noir*,
certainly.

Our able manager, Mr. Skinner, had the brilliant idea of forming a Symphony Forum, composed of students from the universities and colleges around the Bay region. It was wonderful for me to feel the enthusiasm of these young people on Thursday evenings and to realize they had filled the huge opera house by their own efforts. It makes me very proud to think that Mr. Philip Boone, one of these eager and intelligent young men, once president of the Forum, is now President of the San Francisco Musical Association.

"I have been told that many of the young ladies of the Thursday evening audience called me 'Twinkle Toes.' That pleased me no end, as I did not want those concerts to be austere and too formal. From the very beginning a relaxed rapport was established between the orchestra, the young people, and myself. I must say, it was very pleasant to receive many of the very pretty girls in my room after each concert. All in all, this Forum was perhaps the most outstanding effort of my seventeen years in San Francisco."

Caro, I too, loved San Francisco and a terrible feeling of nostalgia possesses me at this moment, I assure you. I loved this city, its style, its lavish way of life, its unique situation on seven hills overlooking the Bay, one of the most beautiful in the world. Of course it was sad to leave after so many years. My sadness was mitigated somewhat by the hundreds of letters I received from people who had loved us and our music. I will never forget one letter signed by seventy riders of the California Street Cable Cars, who told me very touchingly they would miss seeing Mlle. Fifi (our little poodle) and me strolling in Huntington Park. Those days are gone forever except in our hearts and memories.

Tel Aviv, Israel
March 1964

Caro:

The Maestro sits on the balcony of our beautiful
suite in the Dan Hotel here in Tel Aviv, his face reflect-
ing immense joy as the rays of the longed-for sun bathe
the alcove. The sea below rolls over the breakwater in
long white plumes, chanting a restful, deep monotone as
it reaches the shore. Maestro's eyes close and I am sure he
feels he has reached the Promised Land.

We came here from Wales. (Previous to our short
visit with the London Symphony Orchestra in that romantic land, we had been for ten days in cold Hamburg,
West Germany, where the Maestro had renewed contact
with the Nord-Deutsch Rundfunken Orchestra of which
he is very fond.) We shivered everywhere. In Wales I
remember especially sitting up all one night to feed six-
pence pieces to a voracious gas-meter, whose appetite
seemed without end, refusing absolutely to give forth
comforting heat unless fed with good coin of the realm
every hour or so. This was in a city with a lovely poetic
name, Aberystwyth.

You cannot imagine my excitement, *Caro,* that cold,
foggy morning at Paddington Station when we boarded
the train, stepped into a warm compartment that had
been reserved for us, tickets marked London-Aberystwyth
in our pockets. I studied the map on the wall, placed there
by the thoughtful British Railways. It showed us in detail
the route our lengthy caravan would take as it crossed
England into Wales. If we wished and had the time, we
could visit Holyhead, Cardigan, Carmarthen, Cardiff and
Carnarvon. (At the last we could see the immense castle

where Charles the Prince of Wales will receive his investiture.) We could visit Pwllheli and Criccieth and cities with stranger, impossible names. Castles and abbeys, cathedrals and great houses, all were there in this country so reminiscent of Brittany, Cornwall, Ireland. These lands are all peninsulas, proudly insular, yet so anciently related that a man from Brittany in France may well understand a Welshman, but a man from London would have a difficult time indeed with the language.

Wales is a land that feels the cruel force of the Atlantic gales, and lives intimately with fog and rain. It is not a land of bright sunshine, such as is this blessed land we are in at the moment, but a land introspective beyond belief. It is a land of poetry and song. A Welshman's voice is raised the year round in praise of the Lord. I really believe the Welsh think the Creator belongs to them, and to them alone, so very ardent are they in their worship. In our train we gazed at the ever-changing scenery, amazed at the immense quantites of sheep and cattle and delighted at the small Welsh ponies that seemed to roam at will over the moors. At last dusk arrived, and Aberysthwyth, and we left our cozy train for a cold city on the Irish Sea.

We gave concerts in Swansea and Cardiff to warmly enthusiastic audiences, who surprised us by stamping and stomping on the floor of the halls until it had a sound of thunder. Maestro said, "Did you hear that? That is real enthusiasm." I answered, "Are you sure? I think their feet were cold." He looked at me in disgust, but laughed nevertheless. He is a wonderful trouper. One never hears a complaint from him. But of course it is I who feed the gas monsters, *n'est-ce pas?*

In the fine Comet plane of British European Airways on our return, I had the opportunity to talk with my seatmate about his short engagement with the then completely new N.B.C. orchestra. This occurred in 1937 before he started his second season in San Francisco. He will tell you of this curious affair, himself.

"As you remember, *chérie*, that year we were at Les Baux. I was preparing my winter programs for my comparatively new position in San Francisco and, as I remember, you and a group of children were occupied with a project of excavation on a rocky hill called Costa Brava where you did unearth some primitive utensils and remnants of neo-Greek vases. It was early in September, I believe, that a boy from the hotel acquainted me with the news that a gentleman from London would call me by telephone at seven o'clock, French time, and that I should descend to the lobby of La Reine Jeanne at that hour to receive the call. I could not imagine who it could be! Well, as you remember, it was a Mr. Fred Bates, a gentleman totally unknown to me at the time. I learned afterward that he had been designated by the National Broadcasting Company of New York to contact me post-haste. He had written to my Paris address and, as I was not there, it had taken him a week to locate me at our hideout at Les Baux. He told me that N.B.C. was forming an orchestra made up wholly of virtuosi musicians chosen from all over the United States. This magnificent ensemble was to be conducted by my old friend, Arturo Toscanini.

"I replied, 'This is a splendid idea, but an orchestra made of diverse elements, such as you describe, will need to play together weeks before it is an ensemble worthy of the Maestro.'

"Mr. Bates agreed. 'That is why I am calling you, Mr. Monteux. The orchestra has been in training for three weeks with another conductor, but it does not play together and we are very worried. It is on the advice of Maestro Toscanini that we are asking you to come and work with the orchestra and give the first two weeks of programs, before his arrival.'

"I answered that I was very busy preparing my San Francisco season, that we were at Les Baux until October, that I did not think I could do it. The fact was, if you remember, neither of us wanted to do it. We were too contented with our life in Provence, and could not envisage leaving it for New York, which we both dislike intensely. He insisted, however, and said he would give me twenty-four hours to consider the offer, that he would call the following day at the same hour and that he hoped I would accept, adding that I could ask any fee within reason. To make a long story short, I decided to ask such a large fee that the powers of N.B.C. would refuse and give me up as an exigent, ridiculous artist who knew nothing of usual American fees." (This unexpectedly proved to be true, because they at once accepted the large fee proposed by the Maestro and, as we learned later, would gladly have doubled it because they needed him so badly.)

"As we were packing to leave Les Baux, Mr. Fred Bates called again and this time said the most unprecedented thing I have ever heard: 'Mr. Monteux, you will receive a letter from the conductor who has been training the orchestra, begging you to let him conduct the first concert of the series, but you must refuse categorically as the National Broadcasting Company insist you are to conduct the first two weeks before the arrival of Maestro Toscanini. I did receive the letter in question, and I did refuse.

"I arrived in New York to find an orchestra made of splendid musicians, but absolutely no co-ordination be- tween groups in the ensemble. We worked day after day and at last presented the first program on November 13, 1937 in the large studio made for the purpose. A nu- merous and extremely eclectic audience filled the rather barren auditorium for this program:

Pasacaglia and Fugue in C minor	Bach/Respighi
Symphony in D, K.385 (Haffner)	Mozart
Psyché et Eros	Franck
Ibéria	Debussy
Till Eulenspiegel	Strauss

"The orchestra played well, and the program was re- ceived with enthusiasm by all who heard it. I gave the second program a week later and felt my work was well done, as the ensemble improved every day. It was time for me to leave for San Francisco and get settled in our new home for the winter and, as we were in a hurry to leave New York, we decided to take a train leaving that evening for the West. That morning, while we were busy with packing, I received a call from the lobby of the Hotel Madison where we were staying, asking me if I would talk to the personnel manager of the orchestra; it was urgent. I asked him to come to our suite and a few minutes later opened the door to a man, obviously overcome with embarrassment and extremely agitated, to say the least.

· "After a few minutes of greetings and conversation on various subjects, he said: 'Maestro, I am sent here by the —boys, who beg you to come to the studio this morning and teach them *La Mer* of Debussy, which is in Maestro Toscanini's first program.' I sensed this was really urgent! An orchestra does not usually beg a conductor to teach them anything, and I knew they feared the outcome of presenting a work to the Maestro, ill-prepared and indeed not known by all the players. Well, of course, I could not refuse and, as you know, worked for three hours that morning on *La Mer*.

"When I left them, I assure you, they knew it. The men thanked me profusely, but I have yet to receive any thanks from the National Broadcasting Company. *C'est la vie, hein?*"

New Jerusalem
Israel
March, 1964

Caro:

It is sad to think that our correspondence is probably over. I hope we may meet sometime in the near future and discuss various aspects of Maestro's life that seem to have puzzled you. I realize my inadequacy as a biographer. Perhaps it is that I live too close to my subject. Certainly my task would have been simpler if I had old programs, clippings, letters and files as sources of information in which to find the whats, whys and wherefores of this life. Unhappily for me, the Maestro has never believed in keeping anything having to do with his career. Even his recordings are relegated to a back closet in the upper rear hall. He says a concert finished is a concert finished and, as it was usually a disappointment to him, he prefers to look forward to the next hoping that it will be superior to the last.

In three weeks, Monteux will be eighty-nine years old. It is definitely an age for retrospection. I feel deeply some good genie contrived this engagement with the Israeli Philharmonic Orchestra, that these few weeks of slowly setting sun be lived in this ancient country where all speaks to the beholder of the past.

Here in King David's city our thoughts have turned time and again to the Psalms and we hear, in spite of modern sounds of the new city around us, the clashing of cymbals, the dulcet zither and the many-stringed lute. In the distance is Mount Zion, and there on its summit is one of the most revered holy places in Palestine, the shepherd king's tomb. From here one gazes at the Old City, now Jordanian territory, and relives the days of King Solomon the wise, the wicked Herod, the Crusaders, the Saracens and the cruel Turks. Here Jesus Christ walked as a boy and as a man. It is this blessed life one dwells on, and Jerusalem old and new becomes an entity in the mind. Three thousand years old, yet for the state of Israel new since 1948.

We sat in the sunshine and talked of the past. First of this land and its people, then of France, of America, of Maestro's life, and his feelings about the eighty-nine years he has passed on this earth. I will write you some of his thoughts as I transcribed them, Caro. This was a touching hour, I assure you.

"Music has been so much my life that I regret, because of its demands, never having had the time to know the other arts as I would have wished to. I feel incomplete.

"Then, too, music has disappointed me many times. No matter how I try, I can never seem to make it sound as I dream it should sound. Is this my fault? It certainly is not the composer's fault. I'm sure Beethoven and Brahms knew absolutely how they wanted their compositions to sound. Have I let them down by my inadequacy? Once in a while I arrive at producing something beautiful from an orchestra, but these times are rare."

*   *   *

"I think perhaps my great joy was in the quartet. Here all was clear and yes, pure, if you wish."

*   *   *

"Because of a certain reticence, I have never known my fellow-men as I should have if I had been a bit more outgiving. I think this shyness was due in part to our strict upbringing at home. In those days children were supposed to be seen and not heard. My mother had six, and all talking at once would have made a terrible 'bracca' in the home. Today the children monopolize most of the conversation at table. There must be a happy medium attainable."

*   *   *

"Many men have impressed me. Many were quite worth emulating and I did emulate them when young. Youth must have its heroes. Of course the first was Benjamin Godard, then Edouard Colonne, then Hans Richter and Arthur Nikisch. I adored Nikisch. He seemed everything I hoped to be. I was very pleased one day when Louis Zimmerman, the old concertmaster of the Concertgebouw Orchestra, told me I reminded him at times of Nikisch. Childish? Maybe. I think it is good—admiration of worth."

*   *   *

"When I was eighteen our quartet, which I had just entered as violist, made a tour of southern Germany and

Austria. I had never travelled that far and was very thrilled by the voyage. In the course of our travels we met many interesting people and saw marvels I had no idea existed. I remember I was amazed by the wonderful baroque and rococo interiors of Bavaria, and have loved this ornate form of decoration ever since."

*   *   *

"It was on this tour I met Johannes Brahms. The older men of the quartet were very excited at this *rencontre*. I regret to say I was too young to appreciate the honor I was receiving; I was too occupied with my part of viola, too impressed by all I had seen and was seeing. You must remember the three others were all twenty-five and thirty years older, looked on me as a talented youth and saw to it that I played my part as they wished. All I remember of Brahms is a sense of strength, a beard, and rather sad eyes. I was definitely not too impressed. How I wish I had spoken to him in his language! Even now, I find German terribly difficult. Well, I speak with him through his music. He is my love and my ideal. I hope he knows it and forgives the boy who had the serious fault of being too young." (*Caro*, the Maestro's study is full of rare Brahms memorabilia. When he opens his eyes in the morning, there is Johannes Brahms at his piano on the wall before him. I have to smile, because poor Beethoven is relegated to a place just over his bed. I told him one day the great Ludwig would take his revenge and fall on his head while he slept.)

*   *   *

"I can never get over my love for Richard Wagner. I mean, his music. It haunts me and at times I feel possessed by it. This has gone on for years—since I was fifteen."

* * *

"I have always admired Maurice Chevalier. It has filled me with joy to watch him hold the stage alone for two or three hours, sure of himself and sure of his public. He obviously loves them, and they certainly adore him. How wonderful it is to be able to give others such happiness!"

* * *

"There was a great gentleman in San Francisco, Judge Max Sloss by name. For years I looked upon him with almost a sort of reverence. His knowledge of all things worthwhile, his patience in his daily life, his benevolence. He was kind, and his kindness showed in many ways, but particularly in his marvellous visage. I loved him and perhaps he never knew it. Why did I not tell him so?"

* * *

"How I regret not having told César Franck of my profound admiration for him and his music. After playing the Sonata for violin and piano for the first time, I nearly wept over certain phrases. The beauty of it overwhelmed me. I have always experienced terrible emotion in Brahms music, and cannot hear much of it without a mixed feeling of immense joy and immense pain. The slow movement of Beethoven's fourth piano concerto affects me deeply."

* * *

"Young conductors talk too much. I do not know if it is from a sort of nervous reaction, or if they feel the need of showing their great erudition to the orchestra. They do not realize until too late that it was a waste of time and breath. At my age one knows that talk, talk, talk is superfluous. The world is full of people today, all expounding their views on everything under the sun. I wonder what would happen if a week's silence was imposed by law on the populations of all countries. At least it would be a week of quiet, and perhaps a revelation to most people who never take time from their incessant chatter for a bit of introspection."

*   *   *

"I have deplored the fact that many young conductors of our day employ their noble *métier* for self-aggrandizement. Many of them seem to feel the need to make a sort of show of themselves. I think these often erotic gyrations are an insult to their orchestra and most certainly an outrageous disrespect to the music they are supposed to interpret. I have been deeply offended for the composer and have felt like crying out wrathfully, 'Stop!' "

*   *   *

"I have always felt rather badly for orchestra musicians, especially the stringed instrument player who certainly in his youth expected to be a virtuoso and to make a splendid career. I admire their patience and ability, and through the years have made the effort to show them my respect and—love, in many instances. I think they have sensed this sincere feeling in me."

*   *   *

"I am very old and tired, but I love life and hope to live a bit more."

*   *   *

"I deeply regretted the death of Arthur Schnabel. I admired his ideas on music and felt close to him musically. Many of his pupils have become my friends. Do they sense this comprehension of their master in me?"

"In quite another way I feel very close musically to Rudolf Serkin who has played often with me. We always seem to establish a passionate *entente* for the music and it gives me joy, I assure you."

* * *

"I hope you understand me, but it is my feeling that music interpretation has become 'too slick' and too much stress is on technique and too little on taste, and on understanding the *partition* (score). Yes, that is it. There is a lack of taste in the young musician of today. I felt it recently when a young pianist who had been praised by critics for his interpretation of Bartok played a concert of Mozart with me. The fingers played the notes, but Mozart with his charming moments, his *ésprit* and adorable *éspieglerie*, his youthful romanticism, were simply not there. I felt, 'What a dull fellow this is.' What a pity!"

* * *

"I suppose I am what one would call romantic, or *romanesque*. I always dreamed in my youth of a great, consuming love. I was often disappointed and returned each time to my music for consolation. It never failed me. I think you have been a bit jealous of this mistress of mine, *chérie*. You need not be. We have had over forty years of love and companionship together. I am more than thankful to you. Without you, I could not have persisted.

"The hours you have read to me, our drives through

the beautiful Maine countryside, my walks in Meditation Walk at home, our few but dear friends, our various pet doggies, the birds at Winterhaven, the love of our good Hancock folks, all these things and many more, added to my music, have given me a very full life. God has been more than generous with me, I think. I shall be eighty-nine years old in a few weeks. Many things have happened in my world in those years since 1875. I saw the first electric light in Paris, the first automobile. I saw the Tour Eiffel being built. I saw the first gramophone, the first cinema, the first *avion* .... Oh, how many firsts, too many to mention!

"You may think I am asking too much, but I would like to see just a few more 'firsts' before I leave this planet. Do not fear, though. When it is my time to go, I will go peacefully. It will be another adventure. After all, we live toward death. It is our ultimate goal, *n'est-ce pas?*"

VI

IT'S ALL

IN THE MUSIC

*"I do not ask the wounded person
how he feels . . . I, myself, became
the wounded person."*
—WHITMAN

Caro:

Our Maestro has at last attained the goal he spoke of
many times throughout his long life. For ten weeks he
lay in a state of quiescent expectation in his old four-
poster bed ("my own good bed") here in his room at
Winterhaven, this simple home he cherished and delighted in, waiting, waiting.

After the completion in February of this year, 1964,
of a series of recordings with the Nord Deutsch Rundfunken Orchestra in Hamburg Germany, we went on to
Tel Aviv for four concerts with the famous Israeli Philharmonic Orchestra, an ensemble he had longed to know
for many years. He was very happy to be in Israel, contented with the orchestra, and thrilled by the exuberance
of the little country's population. I will never forget the
joy and profound emotion he manifested when his sharp
eyes became aware of the glorious heights of Jerusalem
far in the distance, as we motored toward the Holy City
for our concert there.

From our windows in the Hotel David, the walls of the
old city, strong and indomitable, presented a heart-breaking buttress to the ardent traveller yearning to pass
through the ancient gate. Maestro stood for minutes
watching the sun set on the forbidden city, so near and

yet so distressingly unattainable. At last, in resignation tinged with exasperation, he turned and said, "Those gates are bound to open, I know." Then he returned to his music, smiled, and affirmed with obvious satisfaction, "Well, I'm glad I play Brahms here!" I knew he felt only the music of his beloved Brahms worthy of this great event in his life. That night, the orchestra played brilliantly and he was elated with his Brahms Fourth Symphony, dedicated in his mind to old Jerusalem and the spectres from Biblical times he conjured from the past, feeling no doubt that by the medium of radio he had defied the Jordanian government and had traversed the great wall with his music. We returned reluctantly to Tel Aviv, packed our luggage and flew to Rome the following day, sad to leave Palestine and its valiant people who had shown him love and appreciation.

In Rome, the Santa Cecilia Orchestra greeted the Maestro with cheers. He was an old friend to most of the men in the ensemble and also a member of the Academia Santa Cecilia. We both felt very much at home in the Sala di Vaticano, the beautiful concert hall where the orchestra gives its concerts.

The first concert Maestro conducted went very well, and we looked forward to the second with pleasure. I felt the restful afternoons in Tel Aviv had worked wonders for his health. He was tanned a ruddy brown, and seemed full of a new vitality after the winter's harsh weather and tiring voyages which had debilitated him somewhat. I congratulated myself on having accepted the Israeli engagement, and was very happy. . . . Then the unexpected happened!

In the first part of the second concert, the lovely, youthful first symphony of Beethoven was a joy for the listener. The Maestro seemed full of the very spirit of youth as he conducted it. He was relaxed and gay during the intermission, and after the fifteen-minute rest period, he returned to the hall for the second part of the concert, the *Pavane pour une Infante défunte* of Maurice Ravel, and *La Mer* of Claude Debussy. Oh, Caro, after very few measures of the *Pavane*, our Maestro slipped backward off the podium and to my horror fell heavily to the floor of the hall, a drop of four or five feet! I ran to him knowing that this was due to a circulatory trouble that had caused him grave discomfort, and worry for us both, for many years. I insisted he be raised to a sitting position, using my smelling salts, and vigorously massaged his neck while a friend rubbed his wrists. He recovered quickly and in spite of vociferous cries from the Roman public that he discontinue the concert, insisted on finishing the program. He played the little *Pavane* which had been so rudely interrupted, then continued with a superb rendition of *La Mer*, in which he seemed to find within himself an extra source of joyous energy, so extraordinarily vivid and grandiose was it. The auditors gave him a tremendous ovation and the Italian newspapers the following day praised his gallant courage.

That night he slept soundly and well, and we decided in the morning to visit Ostia Antica. I called our chauffeur and we drove toward the sea and lunched at a quaint fish restaurant there, proceeding on to the ruins in the afternoon. We strolled for an hour in the grassy paths between the fantastic vestiges of that city of antiquity so near to modern Rome. For a while a press photographer followed us and Maestro, who was in fine fettle, whispered: "Look very cross, and scare him away!" This command I obeyed and, to his great amusement, it worked beautifully. We lingered on in Rome for a few days, and left on April third for Assisi by motor car.

Many times during the winter the Maestro had expressed the wish to pass his eighty-ninth birthday "with Saint Francis," the holy one of Assisi he so revered. We had a most enjoyable drive and arrived in the wonderful little Umbrian town on the slope of Mount Subasio refreshed in spirit by the beautiful Italian countryside. We dined lightly, discussed the pleasant day and prepared for bed. Then, just as Maestro seemed ready for sleep, he gave a faint cry and left me, for what to me appeared an eternity. I could not leave him to call for help, and concentrated on massage, medicine, and prayer, and at last brought him to. He went immediately off to sleep. I was very anxious and watched over him the greater part of the night.

He slept ten full hours and woke up to a new day, his birthday, fresh and happy. We had a gay breakfast, I made a flowery speech and presented him with the little gift I had bought in Rome for the occasion. At ten o'clock we drove down the valley to the Basilica of St. Mary of the Angels. Maestro could not wait to visit the tiny Portiuncula oratory of the good Saint, and was ardent in his desire to stand a while in the cell where the holy one died. He went directly to the chapel and there I left him deep in meditation and contemplation.

Knowing the cathedral well, having visited it often over the years, I decided to attend Mass with a group of straggling, uncombed English school girls on Easter holiday. They were quiet and devout during Mass and I was somehow comforted by their young presence. It seemed a good omen, and I prayed Maestro would have a fine ninetieth year, free from worry and sickness. When Mass

was over, I returned to the Portiuncula and found
Maestro lost in prayer. I sat down behind him and waited.
He took no notice of me and I decided, as it was cold in
the oratory, that we should leave. I tapped him lightly
on the shoulder and whispered, "You have been here
fifty minutes, *cher*, and we must go, it is chilly." We
knelt before the primitive small altar a few minutes and
reluctantly left the blessed place—I little thought—forever.

On our way to Perugia where we were to have a festive
luncheon, I took his hand in mine and in a tone purposely
light, said, "Darling, did you have so much to pray for,
you who are so good?"

He smiled and answered simply, "I was asking God
to please give me just one more year with my beautiful
music, just till my ninetieth birthday." The lump in my
throat prevented me from answering.

Our birthday luncheon was perfect and Maestro enjoyed every minute of it. As it was raining that afternoon, we returned to Assisi and the Hotel Fontebella for
rest. At five o'clock the telephone rang and we were told
that the young Mayor of Assisi had come to call on the
old Maestro. We went down to the salon immediately,
were presented to His Honor, listened to a fine speech,
were given a bouquet of flowers, and glass after glass of
Italian champagne. (Served very cold, it pleases me but
the Maestro has always compared it to apple juice!) We
drank to a wonderful year, to his health and success,
thanked His Honor for coming, and I then put a tired
but happy Maestro to bed. He was contented with his day,
and told me it was one of the nicest birthdays he had ever
had. That night he again slept ten hours.

The following morning we left for Milano by car. It

was a beautiful, shining day after the rain. We were entranced by the play of sunlight on the mountain villages and the Maestro told the chauffeur to stop many times as we journeyed through the picturesque Italian country. The lovely voyage seemed much too short and we arrived at Milan filled with regret that it was over and that work would start the very next morning.

The rehearsals with R.A.I. the Italian Radio orchestra were arduous and annoying. The taxing *Fantastic Symphony* of Hector Berlioz, fifty-five minutes long, was the final number on the program. Preceding this discursive work, were the overture to *The Flying Dutchman* and the double concerto for violin and cello of Brahms! The Maestro was very tired after every rehearsal and spent the afternoon hours asleep on the balcony of our suite in the Principe e Savoia Hotel.

The concert went off with verve and a sort of eagerness on the part of conductor and orchestra to present their best to the audience in the hall, and to the huge television public in middle and southern Europe. Maestro whispered to me as he passed me his baton and returned again and again to the stage to receive the applause and approbation of the Milan public after the thrilling final movement of the *Fantastic Symphony*, "Well darling, I made it, didn't I?" He certainly did, it was an exciting concert. The press, the following day, wrote of his youthful, vibrant interpretations!

The morning of April thirteen, the day after the R.A.I. concert, Maestro fell backward on the marble floor of his bathroom. He had just finished shaving. I heard the terrible impact of his poor head as it hit the floor. I was long, long minutes bringing him to, and after administering his medicine and an injection in the muscle of his arm, I managed to carry him to the bed with difficulty. He slept soundly half the day. His pulse was normal and he breathed lightly and rhythmically. I sat near him and read. We had a light dinner on the balcony and he asked me to read aloud from the day's newspapers. We talked over all the alarming world events and went to bed near midnight—Maestro to sleep, your correspondent, Caro, to lie awake far into the early morning hours.

On awaking, he announced he never felt better and insisted on motoring to Sirmione on the Lago di Garda for luncheon. He was happy to see old friends in Sirmione and on our way back to Milan decided to visit the two glorious old churches in Alto Bergamo he has always adored. We have been to see these magnificent edifices every year since 1947, so profound was his attachment for them. It was a day of keen enjoyment for us both, a day I shall never forget.

We left for London the day after, sad as usual to leave our beloved Italy. While paying our bill at the Principe e Savoia that morning, I was startled by hearing a cry and commotion behind me. As I turned quickly, the cashier said: "A man has fainted, I guess." It was Maestro! He was carried by porters to an arm chair, I loosened his collar, used my smelling salts and he recovered immediately. After a few minutes, we walked slowly to the terrace where he sat in the good cool air a full half hour before our departure to the airport. Once there he walked to the plane and we made the arrival in London without incident.

That evening I begged him to cancel the London concerts, go home to Maine, see his Doctor Edward O'Meara whom he loved, take a good rest and prepare for his summer concerts in July and August with the Boston Symphony Orchestra at Tanglewood. He refused to listen, crying incessantly, "What! Give up my beautiful programs, my music, my orchestra. Never!" Then, "I was fine in Tel Aviv, I gave fine concerts in Rome and Milano, I shall give wonderful ones here in London with my own orchestra . . . and they count absolutely on me, now please stop worrying." I said nothing.

Four days after that discussion, Maestro had his last rehearsal with the London Symphony Orchestra. They worked on the "New World" Symphony of Anton Dvorak. He corrected mistakes in the parts, delighting the men in the ensemble, as they had played on these same parts for many years. They said to me over and over, "Now we've got our Maestro back, what do you think of him, Madame, correcting those mistakes, isn't that something?" He was delighted to be with his "children" again.

That night London had a severe blackout due to a grave accident in the main power house. Consequently our hotel elevator did not work and we were obliged to climb the six flights of stairs to our rooms. This we did, very, very slowly. Upon reaching our drawing-room, which was barely lit with three small flickering candles, Maestro fell again on his back, hitting his head on a table edge as he fell. He again left me for what seemed an interminable time. I was frantic, as I had also had a slight fainting spell at the same time due to the effort needed to climb the long stairway. We lay side by side on the floor for an hour or so. It was a ghastly experience. Frantic with fright, I made up my mind in the night to pack our luggage and leave for home on the first plane. I was surprised and relieved when he accquiesed readily to this plan, and I telephoned Emmie Tillet, our manager,

to have her travel bureau procure tickets on the first Pan
American plane flying the London-Boston route. This
line had always been most thoughtful for Maestro's comfort, and they sent a Rolls limousine to the hotel, and we
rode directly to the plane. We were accompanied by a
friend and pupil who has watched over Maestro with
loving care the past few years. The voyage was unevent-
ful. Our dear one slept peacefully, and we landed after
five and a half short hours safely at Logan Airport, Boston. We passed the United States Customs and were
escorted by officials of Pan American to Northeast Air
Lines in an automobile provided by this kindly airline.
The Maestro was very tired, and again slept during the
three hour wait in the northeast waiting room. We arrived at last at Bangor, where our farmer and caretaker,
James Johnston, was waiting for us with our own car.
Maestro was pleased to see him, but did not speak during
the forty-five minute ride home.

I have never felt such sweet relief as when I spied the
old white steeple of the Hancock Congregational Church
and knew that I would have our dear one, safe in his own
good bed, with the fresh Maine air filling the room with
the invigorating smell of sea, fir and balsam a few minutes later. Oh *Caro!* Little did I realize he would never
leave his room again.

On the morning of April 25th, Maestro asked to sit
in his favorite arm chair, a capacious leather one placed
before the window with a lovely view of the garden, the
old garden he so loved. That week the lilac trees under
the roof edge blossomed in profusion, lavender and white.
In the long bed by the ancient wall of field stone, tulips
and other spring flowers presented a gay patch of glorious color, and nearer, almost within his grasp, apple

blossoms, lavish pink and white clouds, fell over the garden lawn in bridal array.

I whispered, "Darling, isn't it wonderful to see our dear garden again?" My heart sank when he answered, very simply, "I did not realize Green Park had so many flowers." I realized then that our Maestro had never left London; never once was he conscious of being in his own room here in our beloved home, and through the weeks asked me continually how I happened to have his mother's picture "here in London," as he lay looking at it for hours on end.

Through radiant sunny days of May and June, we watched him slip away from us. Heartbreaking days of incessant talk of music, and of his London Orchestra which seemed to cause him great worry, as he continually insisted it was time for rehearsal or concert, and that they needed him. Our dear *belle-fille*, Marianne Dumas-Purslow, and I took complete care of him. I feel he was cheered immeasurably by her presence throughout the endless weeks. She is meridional, strong as only a French woman can be in emergency, and spoke his language in soft Provencal cadence.

We lived through hours of anguish in which our patient had three slight strokes and, near the end of life, a cerebral thrombosis. He suffered no pain and though knowing us and recognizing his pupils who came to call, continued in a music fantasia of his own creation. One sad day we heard him cry, "Oh that poor Schumann, that poor, poor Schumann!" over and over, then went on to explain Robert Schumann's grave melancholia. He spoke of Clara Schumann and Johannes Brahms and assured me he was sure Schumann wrote his Third Symphony, the "Rhenish," to prove to Clara his ability to write as great a symphony as Brahms. This bemoaning of Schumann's sensitivity went on a greater part of one afternoon; when evening came, he was exhausted. Another time, he bade us be quiet, saying, "It is *The Marriage of Figaro*—ssh!" We kept very still, hardly daring to move. Then he sang happily with a delightful look in his eyes, parts of the overture and arias from Mozart's opera, in his dear old cracked voice. He was happy, but we wept.

"When I see Brahms, I must apologize to him for the way I have played his beautiful music." This amazing statement was made to his pupil, Werner Torkanowsky, conductor of the New Orleans Symphony Orchestra. Maestro adored Brahms' music above all other, and his playing of the great composer's works always showed this love. In the Netherlands he was called the "Brahmsist." One day he asked for the score of the Brahms *Requiem*. I brought it to him and he held it to his breast with both arms and went off to sleep, evidently comforted by its nearness.

He spoke of *seeing* Arthur Schnabel and Willem Mengelberg and told me one day with a very stern face and with a voice full of decision, "We'll play the Preludes (Liszt) the Mengleberg way." I said, quickly, "Oh, I like the way you play them darling, it's a bit zippier." "No! We will play them the Mengleberg way," he replied testily.

Talk of Handel, Mozart, Bizet, Strauss, Tchaikowsky, Stravinsky, Elgar and Hindemith. We thought it strange he never once mentioned Beethoven, Debussy or Ravel, though he did talk incessantly of Richard Wagner, and once spoke of Franz Schubert, whom he hoped to see. Incessant rambling on about orchestral difficulties, celli, violas, clarinet and brass instruments . . . Music, mu-

sic to the end, the left arm swinging in beautiful ara-
besques, the poor right arm lying paralyzed on a pillow at
his side.

One afternoon, agitated and worried, he asked me in
a barely adubile whisper, "Do they all have crosses?" I
answered, "Yes, of course." It occurred to me he was
thinking of the dead and I knew it would please him to
know each and everyone possessed a cross. He smiled
happily at this information. Later, in the silence of the
night, we heard him sing in a strong voice, *La Marseillaise*. Then I knew he was living the stirring war years of
1914–1916 again. Such poignant moments filled us with
a terrible desolation, almost unbearable; the deep, deep
hurt.

One evening of the eighth week my sister, Charlotte
Michlin, and I were sitting by Maestro's bed, both filled
with profound hopelessness. Of a sudden we were startled
by a horrible change in his countenance; at the same time
he gave a loud, inhuman cry, a hoarse, harsh sound which
filled the room. We watched in an agony of suspense as
our dear Maestro, his face livid and contorted, struggled
with the appalling and dreadful thrombosis consuming
him, his poor slight body tortured by an over-powering
perturbation impossible to control. We had called his Doctor who, arriving a few minutes later, assured us he had
felt no pain and in reality knew nothing of what had
happened. We were limp with the horror of those few
minutes. Less than one hour later, Maestro was again
deep in sleep.

From that irreparable night our loved one lay quiet
for days in what seemed complete lassitude, barely noticing as we administered to him hour after hour. Then,
the day before he left us forever, we three stood at the

foot of his four-posted bed, heart-breaking anxiety binding us in a common bond as we listened to his heavy breathing. Without warning, his eyes opened wide, shining with wondrous light, impossible to describe, our Maestro cried out in a loud voice, "C'EST DIEU!" These were his very last words. We kissed him and stumbled from the room, our hearts too full of deep sorrow, our eyes too full of tears.

Marianne watched over him all that night. At half past four, as a sharp line of rose in the eastern sky bespoke the morn of a new day, his pulse was stilled and our Maestro entered his sweet, eternal sleep.

He rests now in our pastoral Hancock graveyard, where departed members of our family sleep close by. This is where he longed to be, surrounded by the Maine forest, the Bay's water glistening in the distance. Here is the peace he dreamed of, now a reality.

APPENDICES

RULES FOR YOUNG CONDUCTORS
by Pierre Monteux

EIGHT "MUSTS"

1. Stand straight, even if you are tall.
2. Never bend, even for a *pianissimo*. The effect is too obvious behind.
3. Be always dignified from the time you come on stage.
4. Always conduct with a baton, so the players far from you can see your beat.
5. Know your score perfectly.
6. Never conduct for the audience.
7. Always mark the first beat of each measure very neatly, so the players who are counting and not playing know where you are.
8. Always in a two-beat measure, beat the second beat higher than the first. For a four-beat bar, beat the fourth higher.

TWELVE "DON'TS"

1. Don't overconduct; don't make unnecessary movements or gestures.
2. Don't fail to make music; don't allow music to stagnate. Don't neglect any phrase or overlook its integral part in the complete work.
3. Don't adhere pedantically to metronomic time—vary the tempo according to the subject or phrase and give each its own character.

4. Don't permit the orchestra to play always a boresome mezzo-forte.

5. Don't conduct without a baton; don't bend over while conducting.

6. Don't conduct solo instruments in solo passages; don't worry or annoy sections or players by looking intently at them in "ticklish" passages.

7. Don't forget to cue players or sections that have had long rests, even though the part is seemingly an unimportant inner voice.

8. Don't come before the orchestra if you have not mastered the score; don't practice or learn the score "on the orchestra."

9. Don't stop the orchestra if you have nothing to say; don't speak too softly to the orchestra, or only to the first stands.

10. Don't stop for obviously accidental wrong notes.

11. Don't sacrifice ensemble in an effort for meticulous beating —don't hold sections back in technical passages where the urge comes to go forward.

12. Don't be disrespectful to your players (no swearing) ; don't forget individuals' rights as persons; don't undervalue the members of the orchestra simply because they are "cogs" in the "wheels."

PREMIÈRES CONDUCTED BY MONTEUX

compiled by Erich Kunzel

Antheil, George.
Symphony No. 6.
February 10, 1949. War Memorial Opera House, San Francisco.
San Francisco Symphony Orchestra.

Balakirev, Mily Alexeivich.
Thamar, choreographic drama in one act. [Ballet version.]
May 20, 1912. Thèâtre du Chatelet, Paris.
Ballet Russe.

Ballantine, Edward.
From the Garden of Hellas, Suite for Orchestra.
February 9, 1923. Symphony Hall, Boston.
Boston Symphony Orchestra.

Bingham, Seth.
Passacaglia for Orchestra, opus 10
January 21, 1921. Symphony Hall, Boston.
Boston Symphony Orchestra.

Bliss, Arthur.
Hymn to Apollo.
November 28, 1926. Concertgebouw, Amsterdam.
Amsterdam Concertgebouw Orchestra.

Bloch, Ernest.
Evocations.

February 11, 1938. War Memorial Opera House, San Francisco.
San Francisco Symphony Orchestra.

Bosmans, Henriette.
Concertino for Piano and Orchestra.
January 10, 1929. Concertgebouw, Amsterdam.
Amsterdam Concertgebouw Orchestra.
Henriette Bosmans, piano.

Converse, Frederick Shepherd.
"Song of the Sea": Tone Poem for Orchestra after the Poem by Walt Whitman "On the Beach at Night" from "Sea Drift."
April 18, 1924. Symphony Hall, Boston.
Boston Symphony Orchestra.
Symphony [No. 1] in C minor.
January 30, 1920. Symphony Hall, Boston.
Boston Symphony Orchestra.
Symphony No. 2 in E.
April 21, 1922. Symphony Hall, Boston.
Boston Symphony Orchestra.

Creston, Paul.
Dance Variations for Soprano and Orchestra, opus 30.
June 20, 1961. Lewisohn Stadium, New York.
Stadium Symphony Orchestra.
Roberta Peters, soprano.

Culmell, Joaquin Nin.
Piano Concerto.
[In the 1951/52 concert season; an out-of-town concert.]
San Francisco Symphony Orchestra.
Joaquin Nin Culmell, piano.

Debussy, Claude.
L'Après-midi d'un faune, tableau chorégraphique. [Ballet version.]
May 29, 1912. Théâtre du Châtelet, Paris.
Ballet Russe.
Gigue. Casino de Paris. 1913.

Jeux, poème dansé.
May 15, 1913. Théâtre des Champs-Elysées.
Ballet Russe.
Marche Écossaise. 1913.

Devreese, Godefroid.
Tombelène, Ballet sur une l'égende celtique.
December 18, 1927. Concertgebouw, Amsterdam.
Amsterdam Concertgebouw Orchestra.

Farwell, Arthur.
Symbolistic Study No. 3: "Once I Passed Through a Populous City" (after the poem by Walt Whitman), for Orchestra.
March 30, 1928. Academy of Music, Philadelphia.
Philadelphia Orchestra.

Fock, Dirk.
Ein hohes Lied, for narrator and voice with orchestra.
October 30, 1930. Concertgebouw, Amsterdam.
Amsterdam Concertgebouw Orchestra.

Françaix, Jean.
Fantasie for Violoncello and Orchestra.
1934. Paris.
Paris Symphony Orchestra.
Maurice Maréchal, violoncello.
Symphony.
November 6, 1932. Paris.
Paris Symphony Orchestra.

Gilbert, Henry Franklin Belknap.
The Dance in Place Congo.
March 23, 1918. Metropolitan Opera House, New York.
Metropolitan Opera.
Indian Sketches.
March 4, 1921. Symphony Hall, Boston.
Boston Symphony Orchestra.
Nocturne for Orchestra.
March 16, 1928. Academy of Music, Philadelphia.
Philadelphia Orchestra.

Griffes, Charles Tomlinson.
*The Pleasure-Dome of Kubla Khan (after the poem of S. T.
Coleridge), opus 8.*
November 28, 1919. Symphony Hall, Boston.
Boston Symphony Orchestra.

Harris, Roy.
Ode to Truth.
March 9, 1941. Memorial Church, Stanford University, Stanford.
San Francisco Symphony Orchestra.

Hill, Edward Burlingame.
*"The Fall of the House of Usher," Poem for Orchestra (after
the story by Poe), opus 27.*
October 29, 1920. Symphony Hall, Boston.
Boston Symphony Orchestra.
Waltzes for Orchestra.
February 24, 1922. Symphony Hall, Boston.
Boston Symphony Orchestra.

Jacobi, Frederick.
Ode.
February 12, 1943. War Memorial Opera House, San Francisco.
San Francisco Symphony Orchestra.
Symphony in C.
April 1, 1948. War Memorial Opera House, San Francisco.
San Francisco Symphony Orchestra.

Kohs, Ellis.
Symphony No. 1.
January 3, 1952. War Memorial Opera House, San Francisco.
San Francisco Symphony Orchestra.

Lee, Dai-Keong.
Symphony No. 2.
March 13, 1952. War Memorial Opera House, San Francisco.
San Francisco Symphony Orchestra.

Leginska, Ethel.
Two Short Pieces for Orchestra.
February 29, 1924. Symphony Hall, Boston.
Boston Symphony Orchestra.

Loeffler, Charles Martin.
Irish Fantasies for Voice and Orchestra.
March 10, 1922. Symphony Hall, Boston.
Boston Symphony Orchestra.
John McCormack, tenor.

Malipiero, G. Francesco.
Concerto for Violin and Orchestra.
March 5, 1933. Concertgebouw, Amsterdam.
Amsterdam Concertgebouw Orchestra.
Viola Mitchell, violin.

Mason, Stuart.
Rhapsody on a Persian Air for Orchestra with Pianoforte Obbligato.
April 22, 1921. Symphony Hall, Boston.
Boston Symphony Orchestra.
Stuart Mason, piano.

Mengelberg, Rudolf.
Scherzo sinfonico, opus 14.
January 7, 1926. Concertgebouw, Amsterdam.
Amsterdam Concertgebouw Orchestra.
Symphonische Varietés, for Violoncello and Orchestra.
November 20, 1927. Concertgebouw, Amsterdam.
Amsterdam Concertgebouw Orchestra.

Milhaud, Darius.
Concerto for Viola and Orchestra.
December 15, 1929. Concertgebouw, Amsterdam.
Amsterdam Concertgebouw Orchestra.
Paul Hindemith, viola.
Opus Americanum No. 2 (Moses) : Ballet Suite.
1943. San Francisco.
San Francisco Symphony Orchestra.

O'Connell, Charles.

> *Pièce héroïque.* Music by Cesar Franck; orchestrated by O'Connell.
>
> February 21, 1941. War Memorial Opera House, San Francisco.
>
> San Francisco Symphony Orchestra.

Pijper, Willem.

> *Concerto No. 2 for Piano and Orchestra.*
>
> December 22, 1927. Concertgebouw, Amsterdam.
>
> Amsterdam Concertgebouw Orchestra.
>
> Willem Pijper, piano.
>
> *Halewijn,* symphonic drama in nine scenes.
>
> June 13, 1933. Stadsschouwberg, Amsterdam.
>
> The Wagner Society.
>
> Utrechts State Orchestra.
>
> Sydney de Vries in the title-role.
>
> *Symphony No. 3.*
>
> October 28, 1926. Concertgebouw, Amsterdam.
>
> Amsterdam Concertgebouw Orchestra.

Poulenc, Francis.

> *Concert Champêtre,* for Harpsichord and Orchestra.
>
> May 3, 1929. Salle Pleyel, Paris.
>
> Paris Symphony Orchestra.
>
> Wanda Landowska, harpsichord.

Prokofiev, Sergei.

> *Overture in B-flat, opus 42.* [Second version, for full orchestra.]
>
> December 18, 1930. Salle Pleyel, Paris.
>
> Paris Symphony Orchestra.
>
> *Symphony No. 3 in C minor, opus 44.*
>
> May 17, 1929. Salle Pleyel, Paris.
>
> Paris Symphony Orchestra.

Ravel, Maurice.

> *Daphnis et Chloë.*
>
> June 8, 1912. Théâtre du Châtelet.
>
> Ballet Russe

Tzigane, Rhapsody for Violin with Orchestra.
October 19, 1924. Concertgebouw, Amsterdam.
Amsterdam Concertgebouw Orchestra.

Roos, Robert de
Mouvement Symphonique.
February 8, 1931. Concertgebouw, Amsterdam.
Amsterdam Concertgebouw Orchestra.

Rudhyar, Dane.
Poèmes Ironiques.
Vision Végétale.
April 4, 1917. Metropolitan Opera House, New York.
[At an "abstract" dance recital ("métachorie") presented by
Valentine de Saint-Point.]

Schmidt, Florent.
La Tragédie de Salomé.
June 12, 1913. Théâtre des Champs-Elysées.
Ballet Russe.

Smit, Leo.
Schemselnihar, ballet.
December 19, 1929. Concertgebouw, Amsterdam.
Amsterdam Concertgebouw Orchestra.

Smith, David Stanley.
"A Poem of Youth," opus 47.
November 11, 1921. Symphony Hall, Boston.
Boston Symphony Orchestra.

Stravinsky, Igor Federovich.
Petrouchka, burlesque scenes in four tableaux.
June 13, 1911. Théâtre du Châtelet.
Ballet Russe.
Petrouchka. [First concert performance.]
April [?] 1914. Casino de Paris, Paris.
Concerts Monteux.
Le Rossignol, opera in three tableaux.
May 28, 1914. Grand Opéra.
Ballet Russe.

Le sacre du printemps.
May 29, 1913. Théâtre des Champs-Elysées.
Ballet Russe.
Le sacre du printemps. [First concert performance.]
April 5, 1914. Casino de Paris, Paris.
Concerts Monteux.

Strube, Gustav.
Four Preludes for Orchestra.
November 12, 1920. Symphony Hall, Boston.
Boston Symphony Orchestra.

Tchérépnine, Nicolai.
Papillons, ballet in one act. Music by Robert Schumann;
   orchestrated by Tchérépnine.
April 16, 1914. Monte Carlo.
Ballet Russe.

Weingand, Theodore.
Two Dances from "Crazy House Suite." Music by Jon Cow-
   ley; orchestrated by Weingand.
March 11, 1938. War Memorial Opera House, San Francisco.
San Francisco Symphony Orchestra.

DISCOGRAPHY OF PIERRE MONTEUX
compiled by Erich Kunzel

BACH, JOHANN SEBASTIAN

Concerto for Two Violins and Orchestra in D minor.
Paris Symphony Orchestra
Yehudi Menuhin and Georges Enesco, violins

H.M.V. DB 1718/9	78
H.M.V. FJLP 5018	33
H.M.V. COLH 77	33
R.C.A. Victor (U.S.A.)˙ 7732/3	78
R.C.A. Victor (U.S.A.) 11–8601/2, set DM 932	78
R.C.A. Victor (U.S.A.) set WCT 1120	45
R.C.A. Victor (U.S.A.) LCT 1120	33
R.C.A. Victor (U.S.A.) LVT 1006	33

Passacaglia and Fugue in C minor (Arranged for orchestra by Ottorino Respighi).
San Francisco Symphony Orchestra

H.M.V. DB 21053/4	78
R.C.A. Victor (Italy) A 12 R0158	33
R.C.A. Victor (U.S.A.) 12–1057/8, set DM 1340	78
R.C.A. Victor (U.S.A.) set WDM 1340	45
R.C.A. Victor (U.S.A.) LM 149	33
R.C.A. Victor (U.S.A.) LM 1799	33
R.C.A. Victor (U.S.A.) LVT 1039	33

Suite No. 2 for Flute and String Orchestra.
London Symphony Orchestra
Claude Monteux, flute

Decca (England) LXT 6112	33
Decca (England) SXL 6112	33 S
London (U.S.A.) CM 9400	33
London (U.S.A.) CS 6400	33 S

Weinachts-Oratorium—No. 10, *Sinfonia* ("Pastoral" Symphony").
San Francisco Symphony Orchestra

H.M.V. DB 21054	78
R.C.A. Victor (U.S.A.) 12–1057, set DM 1340	78
R.C.A. Victor (U.S.A.) set WDM 1340	45

BEETHOVEN, LUDWIG VAN

Die Geschöpfe des Prometheus, opus 43—Overture and No. 5, Adagio.
[Hamburg] Norddeutscher Rundfunk Sinfonieorchester

TONO M–503	33

Die Ruinen von Athen, opus 113—Overture.
San Francisco Symphony Orchestra

R.C.A. Victor (Italy) B 72 R0011	45
R.C.A. Victor (U.S.A.) 49–3691, set WDM 1637	45

Symphony No. 1 in C, opus 21.
Vienna Philharmonic Orchestra

R.C.A. Victor (England) RB 16256	33
R.C.A. Victor (England) SB 2127	33 S
R.C.A. Victor (U.S.A.) LM 2491	33
R.C.A. Victor (U.S.A.) LSC 2491	33 S

Symphony No. 2 in D, opus 36.
San Francisco Symphony Orchestra

H.M.V. FALP 114	33
H.M.V. QALP 114 (Italy)	33

R.C.A. Victor (U.S.A.) 12–1004/7   78
R.C.A. Victor (U.S.A.) set WDM 1325   45
R.C.A. Victor (U.S.A.) LM 1024   33

[Hamburg] Norddeutscher Rundfunk Sinfonieorchester
TONO M–2332   33

Symphony No. 3 in E-flat, opus 55 ("Eroica").
Amsterdam Concertgebouw Orchestra

Philips A02247L   33
Philips 835132 AY   33 S
Philips A02393   33

Vienna Philharmonic Orchestra

R.C.A. Victrola (England) VIC 1036   33
R.C.A. Victrola (U.S.A.) VIC 1036   33
R.C.A. Victrola (U.S.A.) VICS 1036   33 S

Symphony No. 4 in B-flat, opus 60.
San Francisco Symphony Orchestra

R.C.A. Victor (Holland) L 16393   33
R.C.A. Victor (U.S.A.) set WDM 1714   45
R.C.A. Victor (U.S.A.) LM 1714   33

[Hamburg] Norddeutscher Rundfunk Sinfonieorchester
TONO M–2332   33

Symphony No. 6 in F, opus 68 ("Pastoral").
Vienna Philharmonic Orchestra

R.C.A. Victor (England) RB 16181   33
R.C.A. Victor (England) SB 2065   33 S
R.C.A. Victor (U.S.A.) LM 2316   33
R.C.A. Victor (U.S.A.) LSC 2316   33 S
R.C.A. Victrola (England) VIC 1006   33

Symphony No. 7 in A, opus 92.
London Symphony Orchestra

R.C.A. Victrola (England) VIC 1061   33
R.C.A. Victrola (U.S.A.) VIC 1061   33
R.C.A. Victrola (U.S.A.) VICS 1061   33 S

Symphony No. 8 in F, opus 93.
San Francisco Symphony Orchestra

R.C.A. Victor (U.S.A.) set DM 1450	78	
R.C.A. Victor (U.S.A.) set WDM 1450	45	
R.C.A. Victor (U.S.A.) LM 43	33	
R.C.A. Victor (U.S.A.) LM 1799	33	
R.C.A. Victor (U.S.A.) LVT 1039	33	

Vienna Philharmonic Orchestra

R.C.A. Victor (England) RB 16256	33	
R.C.A. Victor (England) SB 2127	33 S	
R.C.A. Victor (U.S.A.) LM 2491	33	
R.C.A. Victor (U.S.A.) LSC 2491	33 S	

Symphony No. 9 in D minor, opus 127 ("Choral").
Elizabeth Soederstroem, soprano
Regina Resnik, alto
Jon Vickers, tenor
David Ward, bass
London Symphony Orchestra
London Bach Choir

Westminster set XWN 2234	33
Westminster set WST 234	33 S

BERLIOZ, HECTOR

Benevenuto Cellini, opus 23—Overture.
Paris Symphony Orchestra

H.M.V. D 2060/1	78
H.M.V. W 1141/2 (France)	78
R.C.A. Victor (U.S.A.) 11140/1	78

San Francisco Symphony Orchestra

R.C.A. Victor (Italy) A 12 R0158	33
R.C.A. Victor (U.S.A.) set ERB 5	45
R.C.A. Victor (U.S.A.) LM 1799	33
R.C.A. Victor (U.S.A.) LVT 1039	33

La Damnation de Faust, opus 24—Marche hongroise
(Rákóczy March) from Act I.
  San Francisco Symphony Orchestra

H.M.V. 7 RF 278	45
R.C.A. Victor (U.S.A.) set WDM 1618	45
R.C.A. Victor (U.S.A.) set ERB 5	45
R.C.A. Camden (England) CDN 1005	33
R.C.A. Camden (U.S.A.) CAL 385	33

Romeo et Juliette, opus 17.
  Regina Resnik, mezzo-soprano
  André Turp, tenor
  David Ward, bass
  London Symphony Orchestra and Chorus

Westminster set XWN 2233	33
Westminster set WST 233	33 S

Symphonie fantastique, opus 14.
  Paris Symphony Orchestra

H.M.V. D 2044/9, set M 135	78
H.M.V. W 1100/5 (France)	78
R.C.A. Victor (U.S.A.) 11093/8, set DM 111	78

  San Francisco Symphony Orchestra

H.M.V. DB 6670/5	78
H.M.V. DB 9342/7	78
H.M.V. ALP 1137	33
H.M.V. FALP 118	33
H.M.V. QALP 118 (Italy)	33
R.C.A. Victor (Italy) A 12 R0092	33
R.C.A. Victor (U.S.A.) 11–9027/32, set DM 994	78
R.C.A. Victor (U.S.A.) set WDM 994	45
R.C.A. Victor (U.S.A.) LM 1131	33

  Vienna Philharmonic Orchestra

R.C.A. Victor (England) RB 16215	33
R.C.A. Victor (England) SB 2090	33 S

R.C.A. Victor (U.S.A.) LM 2362	33
R.C.A. Victor (U.S.A.) LSC 2362	33 S
R.C.A. Victrola (England) VIC 1031	33
R.C.A. Victrola (U.S.A.) VIC 1031	33
R.C.A. Victrola (U.S.A.) VICS 1031	33 S

Norddeutscher Rundfunk Sinfonieorchester, Hamburg

TONO M-2357	33

Les Troyens à Carthage—Prelude ("Overture") to Act III.
Paris Symphony Orchestra

H.M.V. D 2061	78
H.M.V. W 1142 (France)	78
R.C.A. Victor (U.S.A.) 11141	78

BORODIN, ALEXANDER

Prince Igor—Act II, No. 17, Polovtsi Dances.
Norddeutscher Rundfunk Sinfonieorchester, Hamburg

TONO M-505	33

BRAHMS, JOHANNES

Akademisches Fest-Ouvertüre, opus 80.
London Symphony Orchestra

Philips (England) A02289L [AL 3435]	33
Philips (England) 835167 AY [SAL 3435]	33 S
Philips (U.S.A.) 500035	33
Philips (U.S.A.) 900035	33 S

Concerto for Piano and Orchestra No. 1 in D minor, opus 15.
London Symphony Orchestra
Julius Katchen, piano

Decca (England) LXT 5546	33
Decca (England) SXL 2172	33 S

| London (U.S.A.) CM 9030 | 33 |
| London (U.S.A.) CS 6151 | 33 S |

Concerto for Violin and Orchestra in D, opus 77.
London Symphony Orchestra
Henrik Szeryng, violin

R.C.A. Victor (England) RB 16168	33
R.C.A. Victor (England) SB 2049	33 S
R.C.A. Victor (U.S.A.) LM 2281	33
R.C.A. Victor (U.S.A.) LSC 2281	33 S
R.C.A. Victrola (England) VIC 1028	33
R.C.A. Victrola (U.S.A.) VIC 1028	33
R.C.A. Victrola (U.S.A.) VICS 1028	33 S

Rhapsodie, opus 53 ("Alto").
San Francisco Symphony Orchestra
Marian Anderson, alto
San Francisco Municipal (Men's) Chorus

| R.C.A. Victor (U.S.A.) 11–8983/4, set SP 13 | 78 |
| R.C.A. Victor (U.S.A.) 11–9500/1, set DM 1111 | 78 |

Schicksalslied, opus 54
San Francisco Symphony Orchestra
Stanford University Choir (in English)

R.C.A. Victor (Italy) B 72 R0011/2	45
R.C.A. Victor (U.S.A.) set WDM 1637	45
R.C.A. Victor (U.S.A.) LM 149	33

Symphony No. 2 in D, opus 73.
San Francisco Symphony Orchestra

R.C.A. Victor (U.S.A.) 11–9237/40, set DM 1065	78
R.C.A. Victor (U.S.A.) set WDM 1065	45
R.C.A. Victor (U.S.A.) LM 1173	33

Vienna Philharmonic Orchestra

R.C.A. Victor (England) RB 16241	33
R.C.A. Victor (England) SB 2110	33 S
R.C.A. Victor (U.S.A.) set LM 6411	33
R.C.A. Victor (U.S.A.) set LSC 6411	33 S
R.C.A. Victrola (England) VIC 1055	33
R.C.A. Victrola (U.S.A.) VIC 1055	33
R.C.A. Victrola (U.S.A.) VICS 1055	33 S

London Symphony Orchestra

Philips (England) A02287L [AL 3435]	33
Philips (England) 835167 AY [SAL 3435]	33 S
Philips (U.S.A.) 500035	33
Philips (U.S.A.) 900035	33 S

Variations on a Theme of Haydn, opus 56a ("St. Antoni Chorale").
London Symphony Orchestra

R.C.A. Victor (England) RB 16281	33
R.C.A. Victor (England) SB 2108	33 S
R.C.A. Victor (U.S.A.) LM 2418	33
R.C.A. Victor (U.S.A.) LSC 2418	33 S

BRUCH, MAX

Concerto for Violin and Orchestra No. 1 in G minor, opus 26.
San Francisco Symphony Orchestra
Yehudi Menuhin, violin

R.C.A. Victor (U.S.A.) 11–8951/3, set DM 1023	78

CHABRIER, EMMANUEL

Le Roi malgré lui—No. 2, Fête polonaise.
Paris Symphony Orchestra

H.M.V. L 796 (France)	78

San Francisco Symphony Orchestra

R.C.A. Victor (U.S.A.) 12–0978	78
R.C.A. Victor (U.S.A.) 49–0517	78

CHAUSSON, ERNEST

Poème de l'amour et de la mer, opus 19.
R.C.A. Victor Symphony Orchestra
Gladys Swarthout, mezzo-soprano

H.M.V. ALP 1269	33
R.C.A. Victor (Italy) A 12 R0158	33
R.C.A. Victor (U.S.A.) LM 1793	33
R.C.A. Victor (U.S.A.) LVT 1038	33

Symphony in B-flat, opus 20.
San Francisco Symphony Orchestra

H.M.V. FALP 227	33
R.C.A. Victor (France & Holland) A 630254	33
R.C.A. Victor (Italy) A 12 R0021	33
R.C.A. Victor (U.S.A.) set WDM 1582	45
R.C.A. Victor (U.S.A.) LM 1181	33

COPPOLA, PIERRE

Interlude Dramatique.
Paris Symphony Orchestra

H.M.V. W 1106 (France)	78

DEBUSSY, CLAUDE-ACHILLE

Images for Orchestra Set III.
San Francisco Symphony Orchestra

Complete version.

H.M.V. FALP 174	33
R.C.A. Victor (U.S.A.) set WDM 1618	45

R.C.A. Victor (U.S.A.) LM 1197   33
R.C.A Victor (U.S.A.) LVT 1036   33

Nos. 1. "Gigues" and 3. "Rondes de printemps" only.
H.M.V. DB 6182/3   78
R.C.A. Victor (Italy) B 72 R0019   45
R.C.A. Victor (U.S.A.) 11–8520/1, set DM
954   78
R.C.A. Victor (U.S.A.) WEPR 12   45
R.C.A. Camden (U.S.A.) CAL 161   33

No. 1. "Gigues" only.
H.M.V. DB 11139 (France)'   78

No. 3. "Rondes de printemps" only.
R.C.A. Camden (U.S.A.) CAL 336   33

London Symphony Orchestra

Philips (England) A02323L [AL 3459]   33
Philips (England) 835205 AY [SAL 3459]   33 S
Philips (U.S.A.) 500058   33
Philips (U.S.A.) 900058   33 S

Le martyre de Saint-Sébastien—Four Symphonic Fragments.
London Symphony Orchestra
Roger Lord, oboe

Philips (England)' A02323L [AL 3459]   33
Philips (England) 835205 AY [SAL 3459]   33 S
Philips (U.S.A.) 500058   33
Philips (U.S.A.) 900058   33 S

La Mer.
Boston Symphony Orchestra

R.C.A. Victor (U.S.A.) set ERC 1939   45
R.C.A. Victor (U.S.A.) LM 1939   33

Nocturnes.
Boston Symphony Orchestra

Complete version; with sopranos of the Berkshire Festival
Chorus.
R.C.A. Victor (U.S.A.) set ERC 1939   45

R.C.A. Victor (U.S.A.) LM 1939   33
R.C.A. Victrola (England) VIC 1027   33
R.C.A. Victrola (U.S.A.) VIC 1027   33
R.C.A. Victrola (U.S.A.) VICS 1027   33 S

Nos. 1. "Nuages" and 2. "Fêtes" only.
    R.C.A. Victor (England) RB 6533   33
    R.C.A. Victor (U.S.A.) LM 2651   33

London Symphony Orchestra

Nos. 1. "Nuages" and 2. "Fêtes" only.
    Decca (England) cep 5510   45
    Decca (England) sep 5510   45 S
    Decca (England) LXT 5677   33
    Decca (England) SXL 2312   33 S
    London (U.S.A.) CM 9317   33
    London (U.S.A.) CS 6248   33 S

Prélude à l'après-midi d'un faune.
London Symphony Orchestra

    Decca (England) LXT 5677   33
    Decca (England) SXL 2312   33 S
    London (U.S.A.) CM 9317   33
    London (U.S.A.) CS 6248   33 S

Suite pour le piano—No. 2, Sarabande (Arranged for orchestra by Maurice Ravel).
San Francisco Symphony Orchestra

    R.C.A. Victor (U.S.A.) 11–9684, set DM
    1143   78
    R.C.A. Camden (England) CDN 1005   33
    R.C.A. Camden (U.S.A.) CAL 385   33

DELIBES, LEON

Coppélia—Selections.
Members of the Boston Symphony Orchestra
Alfred Krips, violin

Manuel Valerio, clarinet

H.M.V. ALP 1475	33
R.C.A. Victor (France & Holland) A 630298	33
R.C.A. Victor (Italy) A 12 R 0131	33
R.C.A. Victor (U.S.A.) LM 1913	33
R.C.A. Victor (U.S.A.) LM 6113	33

Valse lente, Thème slave, Czardas only

R.C.A. Victor (U.S.A.) ERA 253	45

Sylvia—Selections.
Members of the Boston Symphony Orchestra
Alfred Krips, violin

H.M.V. ALP 1475	33
R.C.A. Victor (France & Holland) A 630298	33
R.C.A. Victor (Italy) A 12 R0131	33
R.C.A. Victor (U.S.A.) LM 1913	33
R.C.A. Victor (U.S.A.) set LM 6113	33

Nos. 10, 4a, 4b, 16a, 11a and 14b only.

R.C.A. Victor (U.S.A.) ERA 252	45

DVOŘÁK, ANTONIN

Symphony No. 2 [7] in D minor, opus 70.
London Symphony Orchestra

R.C.A. Victor (England) RB 16287	33
R.C.A. Victor (England) SB 2155	33 S
R.C.A. Victor (U.S.A.) LM 2489	33
R.C.A. Victor (U.S.A.) LSC 2489	33 S

ELGAR, EDWARD

Variations on an original theme, opus 36 (*"Enigma"*).
London Symphony Orchestra

R.C.A. Victor (England) RB 16237	33
R.C.A. Victor (England) SB 2108	33 S

R.C.A. Victor (U.S.A.) LM 2418   33
R.C.A. Victor (U.S.A.) LSC 2418   33 S

FRANCK, CÉSAR

Pièce héroïque in B minor (Arranged for orchestra by Charles O'Connell).
San Francisco Symphony Orchestra

H.M.V. DB 6135	78
H.M.V. DB 11117 (France)	78
R.C.A. Victor (U.S.A.) 18485	78
R.C.A. Camden (U.S.A.) CAL 215	33

Symphony in D minor.
San Francisco Symphony Orchestra (1941 and 1950 recordings)

H.M.V. 21442/6	78
H.M.V. ALP 1019	33
H.M.V. FALP 123	33
H.M.V. QALP 123 (Italy)	33
H.M.V. WALP 1019 (Germany)	33
R.C.A. Victor (Holland) L 16171	33
R.C.A. Victor (U.S.A.) 18246/50, set DM 840	78
R.C.A. Victor (U.S.A.) 18251/55	78
R.C.A. Victor (U.S.A.) set WDM 1382	45
R.C.A. Victor (U.S.A.) LM 1065	33
R.C.A. Camden (U.S.A.) CAL 107	33
R.C.A. Camden (U.S.A.) set CFL 104	33

Chicago Symphony Orchestra

R.C.A. Victor (U.S.A.) LM 2514	33
R.C.A. Victor (U.S.A.) LSC 2514	33 S

GLUCK, CHRISTOPH

Orfeo ed Euridice.
Lisa della Casa, soprano (Euridice)
Risë Stevens, mezzo-soprano (Orfeo).

Roberta Peters, soprano (Amore)
Rome Opera House Orchestra and Chorus

Complete version.

R.C.A. Victor (England) RB 16058/60	33
R.C.A. Victor (U.S.A.) set LM 6136	33

Excerpts.

R.C.A. Victor (U.S.A.) LM 2253	33
R.C.A. Victor (U.S.A.) LSC 2253	33 S

London Symphony Orchestra
Claude Monteux, flute

Act II, Scene 2, The Dance of the Blessed Spirits.

Decca (England) LXT 6112	33
Decca (England) SXL 6112	33 S
London (U.S.A.) CM 9400	33
London (U.S.A.) CS 6400	33 S

GRUENBERG, LOUIS

Concerto for Violin and Orchestra, opus 47.
San Francisco Symphony Orchestra
Jasha Heifetz, violin

R.C.A. Victor (France & Holland) A 630291	33
R.C.A. Victor (U.S.A.) 11–9376/9, set DM 1079	78
R.C.A. Victor (U.S.A.) LCT 1160	33
R.C.A. Victor (U.S.A.) LVT 1017	33

HAYDN, JOSEF

Symphony No. 94 in G ("Surprise").
Vienna Philharmonic Orchestra

R.C.A. Victor (England) RB 16242	33
R.C.A. Victor (England) SB 2111	33 S

R.C.A. Victor (U.S.A.) LM 2394   33
R.C.A. Victor (U.S.A.) LSC 2394   33 S

Symphony No. 101 in D ("Clock").
Vienna Philharmonic Orchestra

R.C.A. Victor (England) RB 16242   33
R.C.A. Victor (England) SB 2111   33 S
R.C.A. Victor (U.S.A.) LM 2394   33
R.C.A. Victor (U.S.A.) LSC 2394   33 S

HUMMEL, JOHANN

Concerto for Trumpet and Orchestra in
[Boston Chamber Ensemble]
Armando Ghitalla, trumpet

Cambridge CRM 819   33
Cambridge CRS 1819   33 S

IBERT, JACQUES

Escales (Ports of Call).
San Francisco Symphony Orchestra

R.C.A. Victor (U.S.A.) 11–9907/8, set DM
1173   78
R.C.A. Victor (U.S.A.) 18–0080/1, set V 10   78

d'INDY, VINCENT

Fervaal, opus 40—Introduction to Act I.
San Francisco Symphony Orchestra

R.C.A. Victor (U.S.A.) 11–9509, set DM
1113   78
R.C.A. Camden (England) CDN 1005   33
R.C.A. Camden (U.S.A.) CAL 385   33

Istar, opus 42 (Symphonic Variations for Orchestra).
San Francisco Symphony Orchestra

      R.C.A. Victor (U.S.A.) 11–9104/5, set SP 16   78
      R.C.A. Victor (U.S.A.) 11–9508/9, set DM
      1113   78
      R.C.A. Camden (England) CDN 1005   33
      R.C.A. Camden (U.S.A.) CAL 385   33

Symphonie sur un chant montagnard francais, opus 25 (Symphony No. 1 in G).
San Francisco Symphony Orchestra
Maxim Shapiro, piano

      R.C.A. Victor (U.S.A.) 11–8367/9, set DM
      913   78

Symphony No. 2 in B-flat, opus 57.
San Francisco Symphony Orchestra

      R.C.A. Victor (U.S.A.) 11–8441/5, set DM
      943   78
      R.C.A. Victor (U.S.A.) set WCT 1125   45
      R.C.A. Victor (U.S.A.) LCT 1125   33

KHATCHATURIAN, ARAM

Concerto for Violin and Orchestra.
Boston Symphony Orchestra
Leonid Kogan, violin

      R.C.A. Victor (U.S.A.) LM 2220   33
      R.C.A. Victor (U.S.A.) LSC 2220   33 S

LALO, EDOUARD

Le Roi d'Ys—Overture
San Francisco Symphony Orchestra
Boris Blinder, violoncello

      R.C.A. Victor (U.S.A.) 11–8489   78

LISZT, FRANZ

Les Préludes—Symphonic Poem No. 3.
Boston Symphony Orchestra

R.C.A. Victor (France & Holland) A 630204	33
R.C.A. Victor (Italy) A 12 R0073	33
R.C.A. Victor (U.S.A.) set ERB 5	45
R.C.A. Victor (U.S.A.) LM 1775	33
R.C.A. Victor (U.S.A.) set LM 6129	33

MAHLER, GUSTAV

Kindertotenlieder.
San Francisco Symphony Orchestra
Marian Anderson, alto

H.M.V. ALP 1138	33
R.C.A. Victor (U.S.A.) set WDM 1531	45
R.C.A. Victor (U.S.A.) LM 1146	33

MASSENET, JULES

Manon.
Victoria de los Angeles, soprano (Manon)
Henry Legay, tenor (Des Grieux)
Michel Dens, baritone (Lescaut)
Jean Borthayre, baritone (Le comte des Grieux)
Orchestra and Chorus of the Théâtre National de l'Opéra-
Comique, Paris

Complete version.

Capitol (U.S.A.) set GDR 7171	33
H.M.V. ALP 1394/7	33
R.C.A. Victor (U.S.A.) set LM 6402	33

Excerpts.

H.M.V. FALP 30165	33

R.C.A. Victor (U.S.A.) LM 2058   33
R.C.A. Victor (U.S.A.) SRL 1228   33

MENDELSSOHN, FELIX

A Midsummer Night's Dream—Selections.
Vienna Philharmonic Orchestra

Overture, opus 21
Scherzo, opus 61, no. 1
Nocturne, opus 61, no. 7
Wedding March, opus 61, no. 9
> R.C.A. Victor (England) RB 16076   33
> R.C.A. Victor (U.S.A.) LM 2223   33
> R.C.A. Victrola (England) VIC 1023   33
> R.C.A. Victrola (U.S.A.) VIC 1023   33
> R.C.A. Victrola (U.S.A.) VICS 1023   33 S

Overture, Nocturne, and Wedding March only.
> R.C.A. Victor (England) SB 2014   33 S
> R.C.A. Victor (U.S.A.) LSC 2223   33 S

Ruy Blas, opus 95—Overture.
San Francisco Symphony Orchestra

> H.M.V. DB 4323   78
> H.M.V. 7 RF 123   45
> R.C.A. Victor (U.S.A.) 12–0657   78
> R.C.A. Victor (U.S.A.) 49–0883   45

MILHAUD, DARIUS

Protée—Suite symphonique, No. 2
San Francisco Symphony Orchestra

> R.C.A. Victor (U.S.A.) 11–8977/9, set DM
>   1027   78
> R.C.A. Camden (England) CDN 1005   33
> R.C.A. Camden (U.S.A.) CAL 385   33

MOUSSORGSKY, MODEST

Night on the Bare Mountain (Arranged for orchestra by Rimsky-Korsakov).
Norddeutscher Rundfunk Sinfonieorchester, Hamburg.

TONO M–2361   33

MOZART, WOLFGANG AMADEUS

Concerto for Flute and Orchestra No. 2 in D, K. 314 (Cadenzas by Claude Monteux).

London Symphony Orchestra
Claude Monteux, flute

Decca (England) LXT 6112	33
Decca (England) SXL 6112	33 S
London (U.S.A.) CM 9400	33
London (U.S.A.) CS 6400	33 S

Concerto for Piano and Orchestra No. 12 in A, K. 414.
Boston Symphony Orchestra
Lili Kraus, piano

R.C.A. Victor (France & Holland) A 630225	33
R.C.A. Victor (U.S.A.) LM 1783	33

Concerto for Piano and Orchestra No. 18 in B-flat, K. 456.
Boston Symphony Orchestra
Lili Kraus, piano

R.C.A. Victor (France & Holland) A 630225	33
R.C.A. Victor (U.S.A.) LM 1783	33

Concerto for Violin and Orchestra in D, K. Anh. 294 ("Adelaide). (Arranged for orchestra by Marius Casadesus)
Paris Symphony Orchestra
Yehudi Menuhin, violin

H.M.V. DB 2268/70	78
H.M.V. DB 7723/5	78
R.C.A. Victor (U.S.A.) 8389/91, set DM 246	78

Symphony No. 35 in D, K. 385 ("Haffner").
Norddeutscher Rundfunk Sinfonieorchester, Hamburg.
TONO M–2359   33

Symphony No. 39 in E-flat, K. 543.
Norddeutscher Rundfunk Sinfonieorchester, Hamburg.
TONO M–2359

NOVÁČEK, OTTOKAR

Perpetuum mobile, opus 5, no. 4.
Paris Symphony Orchestra
Yehudi Menuhin, violin

H.M.V. DB 2283, set M 219   78
R.C.A. Victor (U.S.A.) 8383, set DM 230   78

PAGANINI, NICCOLO

Concert for Violin and Orchestra No. 1 in D, opus 6.
Paris Symphony Orchestra
Yehudi Menuhin, violin

H.M.V. DB 2283, set M 219   78
R.C.A. Victor (U.S.A.) 8383, set DM 230   78

RAVEL, MAURICE

Bolero.
London Symphony Orchestra

Philips (England) L02380L   33
Philips (England) 835258 LY   33 S

Daphnis et Chloë—Complete.
London Symphony Orchestra
Chorus of the Royal Opera House, Covent Garden, London

Decca (England) LXT 5536   33
Decca (England) SXL 2164   33 S

London (U.S.A.) CM 9028   33
London (U.S.A.) CS 6147   33 S

Daphnis et Chloë—Suite No. 1.
San Francisco Symphony Orchestra
San Francisco Municipal Chorus

    R.C.A. Victor (U.S.A.) 11–9683/4, set DM
    1143   78
    R.C.A. Camden (U.S.A.) CAL 156   33

Ma Mère l'Oye.
London Symphony Orchestra

    Philips (England) L02380L   33
    Philips (England) 835258 LY   33 S

Ma Mère l'Oye—No. 2, Petit Poucet.
Paris Symphony Orchestra

    H.M.V. W 1108 (France)   78

Miroirs—No. 4, Alborada del gracioso.
San Francisco Symphony Orchestra

    R.C.A. Victor (U.S.A.) 12–1107   78

Pavane pour une Infante défunte.
London Symphony Orchestra

    Decca (England) LXT 5677   33
    Decca (England) SXL 2312   33 S
    London (U.S.A.) CM 9317   33
    London (U.S.A.) CS 6248   33 S

Rapsodie espagnole.
London Symphony Orchestra

    Decca (England) LXT 5677   33
    Decca (England SXL 2312   33 S
    London (U.S.A.) CM 9317   33
    London (U.S.A.) CS 6248   33 S

La Valse (Choreographic Poem for Orchestra).
Paris Symphony Orchestra

    H.M.V. W 1108 (France)   78

San Francisco Symphony Orchestra

H.M.V. DB 5964/5	78
H.M.V. ED 316/7 (Australia)	78
R.C.A. Victor (U.S.A.) 18160/1, set DM 820	78
R.C.A. Camden (U.S.A.) CAE 130	45
R.C.A. Camden (U.S.A.) CAL 282	33
R.C.A. Camden (U.S.A.) set CFL 102	33

London Symphony Orchestra

Philips (England) L02380L	33
Philips (England) 835258 LY	33 S

Valses nobles et sentimentales.
San Francisco Symphony Orchestra

H.M.V. DB 6676/7	78
R.C.A. Victor (U.S.A.) 11–9681/2, set DM 1143	78
R.C.A. Camden (U.S.A.) CAE 216	33
R.C.A. Camden (U.S.A.) CAL 156	33

RIMSKY-KORSAKOV, NIKOLAI

Capriccio espagnol, opus 34.
[Hamburg] Norddeutscher Rundfunk Sinfonieorchester

TONO M–2361	33

Le Coq d'Or—Introduction.
San Francisco Symphony Orchestra

R.C.A. Victor (U.S.A.) 12–0502, set DM 1252	78

Le Coq d'Or—"Cortège des Noces" from Act III.
San Francisco Symphony Orchestra

H.M.V. DB 5965	78
H.M.V. ED 317 (Australia)	78
R.C.A. Victor (U.S.A.) 18161, set DM 820	78
R.C.A. Camden (U.S.A.) CAL 215	33

Sadko, opus 5.

San Francisco Symphony Orchestra

R.C.A. Victor (U.S.A.) 12–0501/2, set DM 1252	78

Schéhérazade, opus 35.

San Francisco Symphony Orchestra
Naoum Blinder, violin

R.C.A. Victor (Italy) A 12 R0077	33
R.C.A. Victor (U.S.A.) 11–8384/8, set DM 920	78
R.C.A. Victor (U.S.A.) set WDM 920	45
R.C.A. Victor (U.S.A.) set ERC 2	45
R.C.A. Victor (U.S.A.) LM 1002	33
R.C.A. Camden (England) CDN 1009	33
R.C.A. Camden (U.S.A.) CAL 451	33

London Symphony Orchestra
Hugh Maguire, violin

R.C.A. Victor (England) RB 16077	33
R.C.A. Victor (England) SB 2003	33 S
R.C.A. Victor (U.S.A.) LM 2208	33
R.C.A. Victor (U.S.A.) LSC 2208	33 S
R.C.A. Victrola (England) VIC 1013	33
R.C.A. Victrola (U.S.A.) VIC 1013	33
R.C.A. Victrola (U.S.A.) VICS 1013	33 S

Symphony No. 2, opus 9 ("Antar").

San Francisco Symphony Orchestra

H.M.V. DB 6918/20	78
R.C.A. Victor (U.S.A.) 12–0179/81, set DM 1203	78

The Tale of Tsar Saltan—Introduction ("Warrior's March") to Act I.

San Francisco Symphony Orchestra

H.M.V. 7 RF 278	45
R.C.A. Victor (U.S.A.) 11–8388, set DM 920	78

SAINT-SAËNS, CAMILLE

Havanaise for Violin and Orchestra, opus 83.
Boston Symphony Orchestra
Leonid Kogan, violin

R.C.A. Victor (U.S.A.) LM 2220	33	
R.C.A. Victor (U.S.A.) LSC 2220	33 S	

SCHUBERT, FRANZ

Rosamunde, opus 26, D. 797—Selections.
Vienna Philharmonic Orchestra

Overture, Ballet I & II, Entr'acte in B-flat.
R.C.A. Victor (England) RB 16076	33
R.C.A. Victor (U.S.A.) LM 2223	33
R.C.A. Victrola (England) VIC 1023	33
R.C.A. Victrola (U.S.A.) VIC 1023	33
R.C.A. Victrola (U.S.A.) VICS 1023	33 S

Overture, Ballet I, Entr'acte in B-flat.
R.C.A. Victor (England) SB 2014	33
R.C.A. Victor (U.S.A.) LSC 2223	33 S

Ballet I & II.
R.C.A. Victor (England) SRC 7026	45 S

Symphony No. 8 in B minor, D. 759 ("Unfinished").
Amsterdam Concertgebouw Orchestra

Philips (England) A02393	33

SCHUMANN, ROBERT

Symphony No. 4 in D minor, opus 120.
San Francisco Symphony Orchestra

R.C.A. Victor (Holland) L 16393	33

R.C.A. Victor (U.S.A.) set WDM 1714   45

R.C.A. Victor (U.S.A.) LM 1714   33

SCRIABIN, ALEXANDER

Poème d'extase, opus 54.
San Francisco Symphony Orchestra

    R.C.A. Victor (U.S.A.) 12–0641/2, set DM
    1270   78

Boston Symphony Orchestra
Roger Voisin, trumpet

    R.C.A. Victor (France & Holland) A 630204   33
    R.C.A. Victor (Italy) A 12 R0073   33
    R.C.A. Victor (U.S.A.) LM 1775   33

SIBELIUS, JEAN

Symphony No. 2 in D, opus 43.
London Symphony Orchestra

    R.C.A. Victor (England) RB 16186   33
    R.C.A. Victor (England) SB 2070   33 S
    R.C.A. Victor (U.S.A.) LM 2342   33
    R.C.A. Victor (U.S.A.) LSC 2342   33 S

STRAVINSKY, IGOR

L'Oiseau de feu—Suite
Paris Conservatoire Orchestra

    R.C.A. Victor (England) RB 16047   33
    R.C.A. Victor (England) SB 2037   33 S
    R.C.A. Victor (U.S.A.) LM 2113   33
    R.C.A. Victor (U.S.A.) LSC 2113   33 S
    R.C.A. Victrola (England) VIC 1027   33

R.C.A. Victrola (U.S.A.) VIC 1027   33

R.C.A. Victrola (U.S.A.) VICS 1027   33 S

Petrouchka—Complete.
Boston Symphony Orchestra
Bernard Zighera, piano

R.C.A. Victor (U.S.A.) FTC 2007   45 S

R.C.A. Victor (U.S.A.) LM 2376   33

R.C.A. Victor (U.S.A.) LSC 2376   33 S

Petrouchka—Suite.
[Paris] Symphony Orchestra

H.M.V. W 1008/11 (France)   78

Paris Conservatoire Orchestra
Julius Katchen, piano

R.C.A. Victor (England) RB 16047   33

R.C.A. Victor (England) SB 2037   33 S

R.C.A. Victor (U.S.A.) LM 2113   33

R.C.A. Victor (U.S.A.) LSC 2113   33 S

Le sacre du printemps.
[Paris] Symphony Orchestra

H.M.V. W 1016/9   78

San Francisco Symphony Orchestra

H.M.V. DB 6804/7   78

H.M.V. DB 9409/12   78

R.C.A. Victor (U.S.A.) 11–9164/7, set DM
1052   78

R.C.A. Camden (U.S.A.) CAL 110   33

Boston Symphony Orchestra

H.M.V. FALP 294   33

R.C.A. Victor (Italy) A 12 R0080   33

R.C.A. Victor (U.S.A.) set WDM 1548   45

R.C.A. Victor (U.S.A.) LM 1149   33

Paris Conservatoire Orchestra

R.C.A. Victor (England) RB 16007	33
R.C.A. Victor (England) SB 2005	33 S
R.C.A. Victor (England) SF 5015	33 S
R.C.A. Victor (U.S.A.) LM 2085	33
R.C.A. Victor (U.S.A.) LSC 2085	33 S
R.C.A. Victor (U.S.A.) SP 3313	33 S
R.C.A. Victrola (England) VIC 1017	33

TCHAIKOVSKY, PETER

Sleeping Beauty, opus 66—Selections.
London Symphony Orchestra

R.C.A. Victor (England) RB 16063	33
R.C.A. Victor (England) SB 2013	33 S
R.C.A. Victor (England) RB 6542	33
R.C.A. Victor (England) SB 6542	33 S
R.C.A. Victor (U.S.A.) LM 2177	33
R.C.A. Victor (U.S.A.) LSC 2177	33 S
R.C.A. Victor (U.S.A.) set LM 6097	33
R.C.A. Victor (U.S.A.) set LSC 6097	33 S
R.C.A. Victor (U.S.A.) set LM 6803	33
R.C.A. Victor (U.S.A.) set LSC 6803	33 S
R.C.A. Victrola (England) VIC 1011	33

Swan Lake, opus 20—Selections.
London Symphony Orchestra
Hugh Maguire, violin

Philips (England) A02261L	33
Philips (England) 610812 VL	33
R.C.A. Victor (England) SB 2093	33 S
R.C.A. Victor (U.S.A.) LM 2369	33
R.C.A. Victor (U.S.A.) LSC 2369	33 S
Philips (England) 835142 AY	33 S

Symphony No. 4 in F minor, opus 36.
Boston Symphony Orchestra

R.C.A. Victor (England) RB 16220	33

Symphony No. 5 in E minor, opus 64.
Boston Symphony Orchestra
James Stagliano, French horn

R.C.A. Victor (England) RB 16161	33
R.C.A. Victor (England) SB 2045	33 S
R.C.A. Victor (U.S.A.) LM 2239	33
R.C.A. Victor (U.S.A.) LSC 2239	33 S
R.C.A. Victor (U.S.A.) set LM 6803	33
R.C.A. Victor (U.S.A.) set LSC 6803	33 S
R.C.A. Victor (U.S.A.) set LM 6902	33
R.C.A. Victor (U.S.A.) set LSC 6902	33 S

[Hamburg] Norddeutscher Rundfunk Sinfonieorchester

TONO M–2333	33

Symphony No. 6 in B minor, opus 74 ("Pathetique").
Boston Symphony Orchestra

H.M.V. ALP 1356	33
R.C.A. Victor (England) RB 16143	33
R.C.A. Victor (England) SB 2024	33 S
R.C.A. Victor (France & Holland) A 630297	33
R.C.A. Victor (Italy) A 12 R0173	33
R.C.A. Victor (U.S.A.) LM 1901	33
R.C.A. Victor (U.S.A.) LSC 1901	33 S
R.C.A. Victor (U.S.A.) set LM 6902	33
R.C.A. Victor (U.S.A.) set LSC 6902	33 S
R.C.A. Victrola (England) VIC 1009	33
R.C.A. Victrola (U.S.A.) VIC 1009	33
R.C.A. Victrola (U.S.A.) VICS 1009	33 S

VERDI, GIUSEPPE

La Traviata.
Rosanna Carteri, soprano (Violetta Valery)
Cesare Valletti, tenor (Alfredo Germont)
Leonard Warren, baritone (Giorgio Germont)
Rome Opera House Orchestra and Chorus

Complete version.

H.M.V. ALP 1419/21   33
R.C.A. Victor (U.S.A.) set LM 6040   33

Excerpts.

R.C.A. Victor (U.S.A.) set ERC 2044   45
R.C.A. Victor (U.S.A.) LM 2044   33
R.C.A. Victor (England) RB 16089   33
R.C.A. Victor (U.S.A.) set LM 6061   33
R.C.A. Victor (U.S.A.) SRL 1228   33

WAGNER, RICHARD

Der fliegende Holländer—Overture.
Tannhauser—Overture.
Tristan und Isolde—Act I, Prelude; and Act III, "Liebestod."
Norddeutscher Rundfunk, Hamburg.

TONO M–2362   33

RECORDINGS BY PIERRE MONTEUX
NOT RELEASED
(*January 1965*)

Beethoven: *Egmont, opus 84*—Overture.
London Symphony Orchestra
R.C.A. Victor

Beethoven: *Fidelio, opus 72*—Overture.
London Symphony Orchestra
R.C.A. Victor

Beethoven: *König Stephen, oder Ungarns Erster Wohltäter,
opus 117*—Overture.
London Symphony Orchestra
R.C.A. Victor

Beethoven: *Leonore Overture No. 3 in C, opus 72a.*
London Symphony Orchestra
R.C.A. Victor (U.S.A.) K2 RY 6806 (33 S)

Beethoven: *Symphony No. 2 in D, opus 36.*
London Symphony Orchestra
R.C.A. Victor

Beethoven: *Symphony No. 4 in B-flat, opus 60.*
London Symphony Orchestra
R.C.A. Victor (U.S.A.) K2 RY 6805 (33 S)

Beethoven: *Symphony No. 5 in C minor, opus 67.*
London Symphony Orchestra
R.C.A. Victor

Beethoven: *Symphony No. 9 in D minor, opus 127* ("Choral") .
  Boston Symphony Orchestra
  [Boston] Pro Musica Chorus
    R.C.A. Victor
    (Monteux's 85th Birthday Performance in Symphony Hall,
    Boston.)

Strauss, R.: *Tod und Verklärung, opus 24.*
  San Francisco Symphony Orchestra
    R.C.A. Victor (U.S.A.) L2 RY 0856 (33 S)

Wagner: *Siegfried Idyll.*
  San Francisco Symphony Orchestra
    R.C.A. Victor (U.S.A.) L2 RY 0857 (33 S)

INDEX

(The *Discography* and *Premières*, listed alphabetically by composers on pages 225–263, are not indexed here.)

INDEX